HISTORIC ROUTE 66

Trivia, Fun & Games

A Playful History of America's Highway

Lana Bandy &
Dale Ratermann

Blue River Press
Indianapolis

Cover designed by Phil Velikan
Packaged by Wish Publishing

Printed in the United States of America
10 9 8 7 6 5 4 3 2 1

Distributed in the United States by
Cardinal Publishers Group
www.cardinalpub.com

Table of Contents

Historic Route 66

Route 66 was established on November 11, 1926, as part of a movement to standardize America's highways. The road, which ran from Chicago, Illinois, to Los Angeles, California, started out as a gravel and dirt path covering 2,448 miles. It also runs through Missouri, Kansas, Oklahoma, Texas, New Mexico and Arizona.

The Route was busy in the 1930s as down-on-their-luck farming families (particularly Okies and Arkies) headed west looking for agricultural jobs. Businesses and communities popped up along the Route and small towns grew. Many mom-and-pop businesses, such as restaurants, gas stations and motels, prospered – even during the Depression – because of the travelers in need of such amenities. By 1938, the road had been completely paved, easing the way a bit.

During World War II, Route 66 was a main thoroughfare for moving heavy military equipment. In the 1950s, it became popular with vacationers on their way to California. This again led to more businesses and attractions – from teepee-shaped inns to reptile farms – as well as road enhancements.

Despite many improvements throughout its years, Route 66 gradually started being replaced by larger, more technologically advanced highways. In 1956, President Dwight Eisenhower signed the Interstate Highway Act, which eventually led to the end of Route 66.

By 1985, the Route was officially removed from the U.S. highway system. No single road replaced it; instead, travelers were choosing to take the interstates that often ran parallel to Route 66. The main roads, still heavily used today, include Interstate 55 (Chicago to St. Louis), Interstate 44 (to Oklahoma City) and Interstates 40, 15, 210 and 10 (to California).

Opposite page: The National Route 66 Museum at Elk City, Okla.

It is no longer possible to take Route 66 all the way from Chicago to L.A., but portions of the road are still open. Quirky businesses, motels and attractions abound. Thousands of travelers drive the Route each year. It has even become a popular summer holiday destination for Europeans who rent motorcycles and hit the Mother Road.

The "world's largest" rocking chair at Fanning, Mo.

Over the years, history buffs have debated Route 66's true beginning and ending points. In 2009, on the 83rd anniversary of the road's opening, a sign marking the "end of the trail" was erected at the Santa Monica pier.

Several Route 66 associations were founded in the 1980s, and the movement to preseve and improve the famous neon signs and motels continues today. In 1999, President Bill Clinton signed the National Route 66 Preservation Bill. This bill gives $10 million in matching fund grants for preserving the historic features on Route 66. Travelers will find Historic Route 66 markers all along the road. While some are traditional black iron signs, others are simply words and symbols painted on the road. One of the most common – the outline of a shield with the number 66 in the middle – has become a worldwide symbol of the open road.

U.S. Route 66 has several nicknames. The Mother Road is a popular one, coined in *The Grapes of Wrath*. The U.S. Highway 66 Association unofficially named it the Will Rogers Highway, in honor of the humorist. Main Street of America is another popular phrase.

```
K B V P O M Z V A W M T R A V E L E R S
A D H O V B D L Y S V J M B D N S W P F
O C U T B C H T B L A E D W E N S B T N
R I B S B K N C Y F R N X V B F X R T P
A R L E T Z K A M I C G J C D C T H C F
D O E D B B K Y C N H F G P A V E N I Q
R T R I C Q O A X W I L L R O G E R S K
K S F S P O N W T P T K Y G R V R Y G N
C I B D V A N H L O E P M A C O T U A O
N H V A H G C G P L C O P S F X S K S I
G X D O D Z H I R X T E J S R U N X A S
V R L R E W O H N E S I E T H G I W D S
U N E R Z S L J L O S K B A S D A A F E
V P V E Z R V P F A M S J T S D M X H R
A K M H N V U W Z O G A C I H C L T X P
Z Q H T U I R E F X A U T O M O B I L E
J J A O M A G V S E L E G N A S O L M D
O L I M T M Q N W U I K E I A W H Z W S
K E T H X C Q A E C Q K V D P S L C J F
```

AMERICANA	LOS ANGELES
ARCHITECT	MAIN STREET
AUTO CAMP	MOTEL
AUTOMOBILE	MOTHER ROAD
CHICAGO	NEW DEAL
CONGRESS	PAVE
DEPRESSION	ROADBED
DUST BOWL	ROADSIDE STOP
DWIGHT EISENHOWER	SANTA MONICA PIER
ENGINEER	THE GRAPES OF WRATH
GAS STATION	TRAVELERS
HIGHWAY ACT	WILL ROGERS
HISTORIC	

Answers on page 133

1	2	3	█	4	5	6	7	8	█	9	10	11	12	13
14			█	15					█	16				
17			█	18					█	19				
20			21						22				█	█
23							█	24				25	26
27				█	28	29	30		█	31				
█	█	32	33	34	█	35			36	█	37			
█	38				39					40		█	█	█
41	42		█	43			█	44			█	█	█	█
45			46	█	47		48	█	█	49	50	51	52
53			54		█	55	56	57					
█	58				59	60							
61	62			█	63					█	64		
65				█	66					█	67		
68				█	69					█	70		

Across

1. Diner dessert staple
4. Payola
9. 4:1, e.g.
14. Genetic inits.
15. State cop speed detector
16. Avoid
17. "___ show time!"
18. Battery terminal
19. Country estate
20. Route 66 moniker (3 wds.)
23. Overshadow
24. Request (2 wds.)
27. Eye problem
28. Invitation letters
31. Capitol Hill worker
32. Computer monitor, for short
35. Rind
37. Firm
38. Earthquake instrument
41. Indian state
43. Buckeye State, not on the Route
44. Health resort
45. Sciences' partner
47. Like some threats
49. "___ the night before..."
53. Sot's state
55. Like the Joliet Jackhammer Giant
58. The Mother Road (2 wds.)
61. Lacked, briefly

63. Sayings from Jesus
64. Partake at a roadside diner
65. Words of wisdom
66. Fable finale
67. Colorado Indian
68. Trifled (with)
69. Stone marker
70. Charley, in Steinbeck's *Travels With Charley*

Down

1. Prepares a pump
2. All together
3. In all likelihood
4. Clutch
5. Talks wildly
6. Admirer of the Route
7. Grow dim
8. Squirrel's home
9. Romulus' twin
10. Site of Will Rogers' fatal plane crash
11. Seafood sandwich filler (2 wds.)
12. Wedding vow (2 wds.)
13. "___ the ramparts..."

21. Family girl
22. Candles
25. Poem of praise
26. No longer working (abbr.)
29. Thread holder
30. Relax (with "out")
33. New Mexico's ___ Puerco
34. Route 66 souvenir purchase
36. Once around the track
38. Part of a weekend
39. Adrian's ___-Point Café
40. Country singer Cline
41. Tank filler
42. Food scrap
46. Mooch
48. Ex-pat
50. Get smart (2 wds.)
51. Fly an airplane
52. Group of six
54. Exposed
56. Kind of skeleton
57. No longer fresh
59. Shade trees
60. Chimney dust
61. Stetson, e.g.
62. *Much ___ About Nothing*

Answers on page 138

Across

7. Gas station name
9. U.S. president who stayed at the El Rancho Hotel in Gallup
10. Roadside restaurant
11. Top prize at the county fair (2 wds.)
12. Middle Easterner
14. Theory of relativity discoverer
15. MPG and Rte., e.g.
17. Drives away too fast (2 wds.)
19. Older siblings
21. Country homes
22. Type of list
23. Rises from a chair
24. Using the copy machine

Down

1. Driver's concern: Gas ___
2. Sore spot
3. "Devil's Rope" (var.)
4. Practice session (2 wds.)
5. Lettuce and carrots, e.g. (2 wds.)
6. Old vehicles
8. Puzzle theme
13. Mound next to the road
15. Road paving materials
16. Cabinet department
18. Woodwind player
20. Sitting in the backseat
22. Car for hire

Answers on page 138

Route 66 Wordsmith Challenge

Seven common words of three or more letters can be made from the letters in the word SIXTY SIX. How many can you come up with? No proper names, abbreviations, slang or foreign words are allowed. Bonus points if you can come up with any of the five words that are acceptable in a game of SCRABBLE, but are uncommon in everyday English. Answers on page 157.

SIXTY-SIX

_____   _____

_____   _____

_____   _____

_____

Geography Trivia

1. What are the three largest cities on the route?

2. What is the biggest river crossed?

3. What is the traditional midpoint city on the route?

4. Which state has the most miles on the route?

5. Which state has the fewest miles on the route?

6. Which five interstate highways have replaced Route 66?

Answers on page 155

Route 66 Sudoku Challenge

Use logic to fill in the boxes so every row, column and 2 x 3 box contain the letters (and numbers) R-O-U-T-E-66. Solutions on page 147.

O					
R			66	O	
66		U	O		
		R	T		66
	66	O			R
					O

			R		T
			O		
E					O
T					66
		T			
R		U			

The Year Was 1926

Can you answer the following trivia about the year Route 66 was finished? Answers on page 155.

1. Who was the U.S. president in 1926?
   a. Calvin Coolidge
   b. Warren G. Harding
   c. Herbert Hoover

2. How many states were in the United States in 1926?
   a. 46
   b. 48
   c. 50

3. Which of these men was born in 1926?
   a. Barack Obama
   b. Fidel Castro
   c. Michael Douglas

4. Which of these men died in 1926?
   a. Harry Houdini
   b. John Dillinger
   c. Charles Lindbergh

5. Which novel won a Pulitzer Prize in 1926?
   a. *Arrowsmith*, by Sinclair Lewis
   b. *The Grapes of Wrath*, by John Steinbeck
   c. *Gone With the Wind*, by Margaret Mitchell

6. Who beat Jack Dempsey to become the heavyweight boxing champion of the world in 1926?
   a. Gene Tunney
   b. Cassius Clay
   c. Joe Louis

Unscramble

Unscramble these letters to form a word or words related to Route 66's history. Answers on page 154.

HERMOT ADRO   _____

XITYS-XSI   _____

I KILE KEI   _____

AWHYIHG   _____

ANIM EETTRS   _____

JNHO CKSTNEIE   _____

Original Route 66 bridge, no longer in use, near Winona, Ariz.

66 Box

Place the numbers 18-26, one per box, so that each column of three numbers adds up to 66, each row of three numbers adds up to 66 and both diagonals add up to 66. We've got you started with the number 23. Answer on page 157.

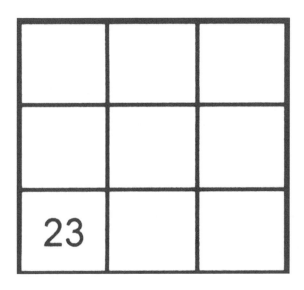

Beware of the wild burros on Route 66 near Oatman, Ariz.

Historic Highway Box

Place the eight states of Route 66 into the grid, one state per row and one letter per square. Use the letters that are given, one per state, so that the letters going down the eighth column spell HISTORIC. Our solution is on page 157.

ILLINOIS		MISSOURI
KANSAS		OKLAHOMA
TEXAS		NEW MEXICO
ARIZONA		CALIFORNIA

						H				
						I				
						S				
						T				
						O				
						R				
						I				
						C				

Roadside Attractions: The Cozy Dog

In Springfield, Illinois, the Cozy Dog Drive-In's claim to fame is inventing the corn dog. Legend has it that Don Strand provided the batter recipe and Ed Waldmire Jr. perfected the creation while he was stationed in Texas during World War II. Waldmire started out by selling the "crusty curs" at the military USO club and PX before he returned to Springfield. Once there, he began selling them at the Illinois State Fair in 1946 under the name "cozy dogs." The next step was a stand outside his house and then a building shared with Dairy Queen.

The Cozy Dog is a popular Route 66 stop. It has a gift shop and its décor predominantly features the Mother Road. Customers can eat in or take their dogs to go. The Cozy Dog is also popular in the media, having appeared on the Travel Channel's Man v. Food program in 2009. The Cozy Dog is currently operated by some of Waldmire's family members, right next door to the original location.

The menu has expanded, and the restaurant serves breakfast, lunch and dinner. A cozy dog is always on the menu at $1.85. Other options include regular hot dogs, chili dogs, chili cheese dogs, cheese dogs, hamburgers, BBQ sandwiches and more.

Illinois

Illinois Landmarks:
1. Ariston Cafe, Litchfield, IL
2. Cozy Dogs Drive-In, Springfield, IL
3. Route 66 Association Hall of Fame & Museum, Pontiac, IL
4. Grant Park, Chicago, IL

Illinois

Traditionally, Illinois was the starting point for Route 66, and it's where many travelers begin their trips today. The Route started on the corner of Jackson and Michigan Boulevards. It curved from Lake Michigan to the downtown Chicago sky-scrapers and through the suburbs and farmlands of the state.

Of course Chicago is the state's top destination. Attracting nearly 50 million visitors a year, it offers such

Hot Dog Giant at Atlanta, Ill.

sites as the Magnificent Mile, the Art Institute and Navy Pier. Some of its most popular sites are on the original Route 66 path. Buckingham Fountain, constructed just one year after Route 66, is the symbolic beginning of the road. It sits in the Grant Park/Millennium Park area. The 1,451-foot Willis (Sears) Tower is the tallest building in the United States. Built in 1973, it was then the tallest building in the world. Other major skyscrapers and historical buildings line the Route 66 path on West Jackson Boulevard and Adams Street.

Popular restaurants in the area include Lou Mitchell's and the Berghoff Restaurant, both of which have served Route 66 drivers (as well as presidents and celebrities) since the beginning. Another unique Route 66 original is the Castle Car Wash, a filling station that opened in 1925. Designed like a (small) castle, the car wash still has a gas station and is owned by a towing company. It was recently cited by Landmarks Illinois (a local preservation group) as a historically significant building in need of preservation efforts.

Leaving Chicago, Route 66 passes through the suburbs of Riverside, LaGrange, Countryside, Darien and Bolingbrook before going through other Illinois towns. Joliet, Wilmington, Gardner, O'Dell, Pontia, McLean, Atlanta, Springfield, Waggoner, Litchfield, Mt. Olive and Staunton are all on the Route 66 path and have several attractions of their own.

Joliet has one of the nation's largest Route 66 communities and often celebrates its connection to the Mother Road with festivals and tours. The town is considered the "Crossroad of America," as it's where the Lincoln Highway met up with Route 66. "The Jewel of Joliet," the Rialto Square Theatre, is located right on Route 66 (or Chicago Street). A gorgeous venue on the National Register of Historic Places, the lobby of the theatre is designed after the Palace of Versailles' Hall of Mirrors. Opened in 1926 (a few months before Route 66), the theatre still hosts concerts, weddings and other events. Other fun facts about Joliet include:

- The very first Dairy Queen opened in Joliet in 1940, located on Route 66.
- The Joliet Prison is where the Blues Brothers movie was filmed, and characters Jake and Elwood can be seen all over town.
- There are numerous historic gas pumps throughout the town.
- The Joliet Jackhammer Giant statue is a huge muffler man dressed in the Joliet Jackhammers baseball team's colors.
- Visitors may want to stop at the Joliet Area Historical Museum to do the "Route 66 Experience."

Farther south in Wilmington, there's another old Gemini Giant statue, this one located at the Launching Pad Drive-

Memory Lane at Lexington, Ill.

In. This restaurant on the north end of town was founded in 1960. The giant holds onto a rocket ship and looks down over Route 66, a typical Mother Road landmark.

Down the road a bit more, travelers venture to O'Dell, a small town where they can see a 1932 Standard Oil Station. The station, restored in 2002, appears just as it would have in the 1930s when service stations lined Route 66.

Just 10 miles south is Pontiac, the home of the Route 66 Hall of Fame. Here travelers can learn more about the history of Route 66, see what it looked like in its heyday, and view paraphernalia from the 1920s to today.

The famous Dixie Truckers Home is a truck stop in McLean. It began as a mechanic's garage that also sold sandwiches to passing motorists. It quickly became a popular full-service restaurant in the mid-1930s. While the Dixie Truckers Home has new owners and a different look, it is still in operation and quite popular, especially among big rig drivers.

Springfield, the state capital, also lies on Route 66. Beside the typical tourist attractions – the state capital building and Lincoln's Tomb – there are several must-sees for Route 66 travelers. The Cozy Dog Drive-In is one of these. The Cozy Dog – a hot dog on a stick – is the restaurant's claim to fame. This delicious treat found at many state fairs was invented here. Another Springfield stop is Shea's Gas Station. Shea's is home to an extensive collection of gas station and Route 66 memorabilia, including old pumps, signs and more.

The Ariston Café in Litchfield opened in 1924 and hasn't changed much since. It's the longest operating restaurant on Route 66, and its founding family (the Adams family) was inducted into the Route 66 Association of Illinois Hall of Fame.

One of the last attractions before entering Missouri is in Staunton. Henry's Rabbit Ranch is in this small town. The ranch is actually a gift shop and information center, though it looks like an old gas station. Outside the building are rabbits galore as well as relics of two old motels and a group of half-buried Volkswagon Rabbits (an homage to the much larger Cadillac Ranch in Amarillo, Texas).

Unscramble

Unscramble these letters to form a word or words related to Route 66 in Illinois. Answers on page 154.

CCHIGOA _____

NTARG PKRA _____

AIRDY EENQU _____

INLLNOC _____

TAIBBR CHARN _____

KNUFS EVORG _____

Die Cast Auto Sales at Williamsville, Ill.

1	2	3	4	5		6	7	8	9	10		11	12	13
14						15						16		
17				18								19		
		20					21					22		
23	24				25	26					27			
28				29					30	31				
32				33		34			35					
			36				37	38						
	39	40				41						42	43	44
45					46		47			48				
49				50	51	52				53				
54			55					56	57					
58			59			60						61	62	
63			64					65						
66			67					68						

Across

1. Fruits with an appropriate name
6. Diner jukebox artist: ___ Hill
11. Backseat game: ___-tac-toe
14. Touch up the wall of a motel room
15. Wrestling's ___ the Giant
16. Cellular stuff
17. Accented musical rhythm
19. Driver's lic. and others
20. Superhero accessory
21. Farm females
22. On the other hand
23. Deuces
25. Route/Boot, e.g.
27. Ship's body
28. Take one's foot off the break pedal
30. Motel bar
32. Japanese currency
33. Fuzzy fruit
35. Merriment
36. Traditional starting point for a Route 66 excursion (2 wds.)
39. VIP's ride on the Route
41. Without a doubt
42. When doubled, a dance
45. Renter
47. Chess champ Bobby
49. Jim Bakker's ex-squeeze,

Jessica
50. Horse's feet (var.)
53. Citrus fruit
54. 401(k) alternative
55. Letter opener
56. Sweeping story
58. Naval rank (abbr.)
59. Shoot the president
63. Dog doc
64. "Same here!"
65. Humidor item
66. Before, in poetry
67. Liability's opposite
68. Use elbow grease on

Down
1. Pkg. deliverer
2. In high spirits
3. Illinois' famous son
4. As a precaution (2 wds.)
5. Red roadway sign
6. ORD watchdog
7. On pins and needles
8. Manner of speaking
9. Gardener's tool
10. Egg producers
11. Chicago daily newspaper
12. Enjoy to excess

13. Royal home
18. Iran, long ago
23. Attempt
24. Teensy
26. Chopped down
27. "The Incredible ___"
29. Goodyear's Ohio headquarters site
31. Fairy tale baddies
34. Part of TGIF
36. FBI operative
37. The Magic Dragon
38. Crops up
39. Trainee
40. A hurried state (2 wds.)
42. The Windy City
43. Skirt's edge
44. "___ we there yet?"
45. Steal
46. Doctoral student's paper
48. Healthcare facility
51. Tobacco kilns
52. Give a speech
55. Early baby word
57. Route trip photos, briefly
60. Drunkard
61. Fraternity letter
62. Misread the map

Answers on page 139

```
G Z V A O N E H C H A M E L F
Z W U D A R I E N G C L G G B
G N T T N U X Z H L W L B A Q
W J F O Y B Z P E O I A T R W
J H D D W U I A O N B N K D W
O K W E R A N D C N A I I N C
Z C I L E Q N O W L T S A E H
X S G L B T L D T R A I V R X
F R H F E N K A A N T M A D Y
D D T I E O K H Z E U P R C V
A Q L D R B K C H I C A G O O
F O R E E L O C K P O R T E N
J I C Q E O E M O R E J G S R
V I U K I W M Y O F M R W J Z
C F Z K R N D K Q X V D B V O
```

ATLANTA	JEROME
AUBURN	JOLIET
BERWYN	LINCOLN
CHENOA	LOCKPORT
CHICAGO	MCLEAN
CICERO	NORMAL
DARIEN	ODELL
DWIGHT	PONTIAC
ELKHART	SHIRLEY
ELWOOD	STAUNTON
GARDNER	TOWANDA
HAMEL	VIRDEN

Answers on page 133

A Little Illinois Trivia

1. What is the name of the restaurant in Chicago that has been serving breakfast to Route 66 travelers since the beginning?

2. The first establishment to sell a corn dog didn't call the cornmeal-covered wiener a "corn dog." What is the delicacy called in that Springfield, Ill., restaurant?

3. What's the oldest hotel on the Route, located in Wilmington, Ill.?

4. Which burger chain's original location is in Bloomington, Ill.?

5. What is the oldest truck stop in the world? (Hint: It's located in McLean, Ill.)

6. What animal is the theme of Staunton Ranch, an attraction that features half-buried cars along with the live critters?

Answers on page 155

Chain of Rocks Canal Bridge, at the Mississippi River crossing

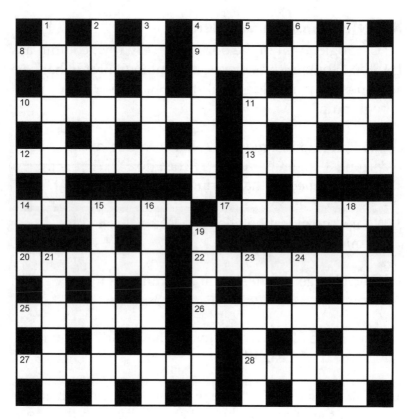

Across

8. Latin American ballroom . dance
9. Route 66 dessert staple (2 wds.)
10. Amorous idealist
11. Came close to
12. BBQ cooking need
13. Running shoe brand
14. Springfield wiener place
17. Home to Route 66 Hall of Fame
20. Famed tenor
22. Like many of the Route's curios
25. Use Listerine
26. Classic car brand
27. Nada (2 wds.)

28. Chocolate treats

Down

1. Train sound, to a child
2. Oblong cream puff
3. Body art
4. Illinois motto: Land of ___
5. Signor da Vinci
6. Hood ___
7. Backyard structure, often
15. Newest
16. Mileage measurer
18. Kool-Aid package direction (2 wds.)
19. Route 66 eastern terminus
21. Web book seller
23. Take a nap (2 wds.)
24. Musical sequence

Answers on page 139

Route 66 Sudoku Challenge

Use logic to fill in the boxes so every row, column and 2 x 3 box contain the letters (and numbers) R-O-U-T-E-66. Solutions on pages 147-148.

R	U	T			
			R		
	O	U			
			E	O	
		R			
			T	R	66

R	O				
U	E				66
O					U
E					O
66				O	T
				66	R

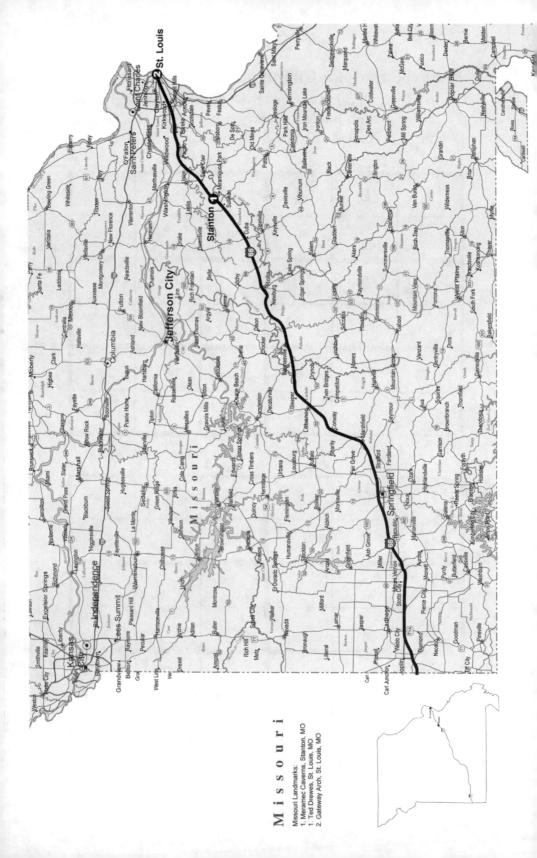

Missouri

Missouri Landmarks:
1. Meramec Caverns, Stanton, MO
1. Ted Drewes, St. Louis, MO
2. Gateway Arch, St. Louis, MO

Missouri

St. Louis, the landmark Gateway Arch and the Mississippi River welcome travelers into the state of Missouri. Route 66 covered 300+ miles in Missouri, and quite a few iconic landmarks remain, as do many scenic vistas. Route 66 often parallels Interstate 44 throughout Missouri.

No trip to Missouri would be complete without a stop in St. Louis. The largest city on Route 66 between Chicago and Los Angeles, the first main attraction for western-bound explorers is the Chain of Rocks Bridge. This bridge, built in 1929, crosses the Mississippi River on the north side of St. Louis. It was Route 66's path over the river but is closed to automobiles today. It now has walking and biking trails and is on the National Register of Historic Places. The most striking feature of this bridge is the 22-degree bend in the middle.

St. Louis is also home to one of the most popular venues in the state – Ted Drewes Frozen Custard. Ted Drewes opened in 1930 and has the distinction of being the only U.S. frozen dessert stand to be open 24 hours a day, seven days a week during the summer. While there are two locations in town, the main shop is right on Route 66 (also known as Chippewa Street). Another unique feature of Ted Drewes is that it offers just one frozen custard flavor – vanilla. But many different flavorings and toppings are available. The most popular treat is a "concrete," or frozen custard blended with other ingredients. Servers prove a concrete's thickness before giving it to you by turning the big yellow cup upside down.

Just 17 miles outside St. Louis, the Mother Road passes through the Route 66 State Park. This 419-acre state park opened in 1999 and offers hiking, biking, canoeing and

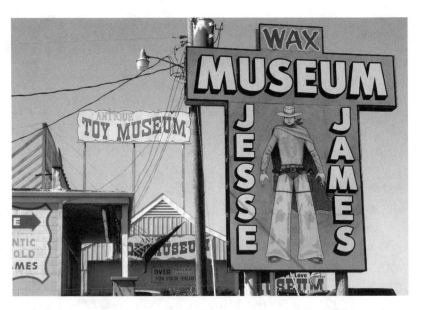

Jesse James Wax Museum and Toy Museum next door at Stanton, Mo.

horseback riding. Turkey, deer, geese, birds and small mammals are found in the park. Part of Route 66 winds through the park, and visitors can see an old bridge across the Meramec River. There's also a museum which features Route 66 and the history of the park. It is quite an interesting history, too. Visitors are often surprised to learn the park was built on the former site of Times Beach, a neighborhood contaminated by dioxin in the 1980s. The town was evacuated and then decontaminated by the Environmental Protection Agency.

Continuing along the Route, visitors reach Stanton and the Meramec Caverns. What draws visitors to these natural limestone caves is the elaborate stalactites and stalagmites that formed during the last 400 million years. The caves served as shelter for Native Americans, runaway slaves on the Underground Railroad and Jesse James and his posse. The caverns opened as a tourist attraction in 1935 and remain one of the premier sites along Route 66. Visitors can't miss them, as there are more than 50 billboard advertisements along Interstate 44.

Legend has it that Jesse James and his gang stopped off at the caverns after he robbed a bank on his way from St. Louis to Little Rock, Arkansas. Lawmen tracked the group to the caverns and attempted to starve them out. But after three days and no Jesse James, the sheriff and his men entered the cave and found only the gang's horses. It is said that the outlaws escaped by swimming to the Meramec River.

Another Stanton attraction is the Jesse James Museum, where visitors can learn more about the outlaw's life, times and mysterious death.

The next major town along Route 66 is Rolla. It was a regular stop for travelers, as it is located halfway between St. Louis and Springfield. Today this town is home to Memoryville USA, a popular car museum and restoration shop, as well as the University of Missouri at Rolla.

A few miles down the road is Waynesville, which has several historic buildings and a quaint old downtown area. The Old Stagecoach Stop was a tavern and boarding house before becoming a museum. It was also used as a hospital for Union troops during the Civil War. Leaving Waynesville, Route 66 travelers often stop at the Witmor Farms Restaurant or the Hillcrest Grocers & Station (service station).

Closer to Kansas, Route 66 travelers may want to visit the following attractions:
* In Lebanon, the Munger-Moss Motel, a vintage auto court that harkens back to Route 66's heyday and features several Route 66-themed rooms.
* Also in Lebanon, Wrinks Market, a community general store that sells takeout, groceries and collectibles.
* In Springfield, the first Steak & Shake restaurant (opened in 1962) and the world's largest Bass Pro Shops. Springfield was also home to John T. Woodruff, one of the Route founders and the first president of the U.S. Highway 66 Association.
* In Carthage, historic Victorian homes and other buildings.

Unscramble

Unscramble these letters to form a word or words related to Route 66 in Missouri. Answers on page 154.

ETAGYAW RACH   _____

EEMMRAC AERCSVN   _____

EEJSS AEJMS   _____

AESTT AKPR   _____

EDLIVS BOWLE   _____

AINST ILOSU   _____

A Little Missouri Trivia

1. Which river does the "Chain of Rocks Bridge" cross?

2. What are Ted Drewes' famous frozen custards called?

3. Who was the architect who designed the Gateway Arch?

4. Where is the world's largest Bass Pro Shop?

5. Which legendary outlaw used the Meramec Caverns as a hideout?

6. What was the name of Jesse James' brother who was also his partner in crime?

Answers on page 155

Across

7. Fancy mustard type
8. It's often rolled out for VIPs (2 ___ wds.)
10. Give a new title to
11. '30s gangster (2 wds.)
12. Phillips 66 product
13. Fencing sword
15. Munger Moss Motel site
17. Cardinals' home (2 wds.)
20. Car for hire
22. Draws in
25. Backyard toilet
26. Subtract
27. Cadillac of campers
28. Bushy hairdos

Down

1. Indian's alcoholic drink
2. Popular soft drink brand on the Route (2 wds.)
3. Missouri cave
4. Trunk soda cooler (2 wds.)
5. Three-bagger
6. 57 Sauce maker
9. Actress Moore
14. Backseat X-and-O game
16. Death notice
18. Switch settings (3 wds.)
19. ___ Arch
21. Struck with fear
23. Type of list
24. Valentine's Day cherub

Answers on page 140

¹	²	³	⁴	⁵	■	⁶	⁷	⁸	⁹	■	¹⁰	¹¹	¹²	¹³

Grid with numbered cells: 1-5, 6-9, 10-13; 14, 15, 16; 17, 18, 19; 20, 21, 22, 23; 24, 25; 26, 27, 28, 29, 30, 31, 32; 33, 34, 35, 36, 37, 38; 39, 40, 41, 42, 43; 44, 45, 46, 47; 48, 49, 50, 51; 52, 53, 54, 55; 56, 57, 58, 59, 60, 61; 62, 63, 64, 65; 66, 67, 68; 69, 70, 71.

Across

1. Take as one's own
6. A single time
10. Doctrines
14. Ebert or Maris
15. Six-stringed instrument
16. Jacket
17. Welsh dog
18. Online retail
20. Load from a lode
21. Wine bottle stopper
23. Hush-hush
24. Pencil component
25. Convertible drivers catch them
26. At no cost
29. Glove compartment item, often (2 wds.)
33. Archaeologist's find
35. U.S. territory
36. Resort
39. Santa ___, Calif.
40. Mother-of-pearl source
43. Witch's work
44. Freight weight
45. Emphatic no
46. Within walking distance
48. Book checked out again
51. TV's "American ___"
52. Christmas tree topper
54. Former
56. Rears

58. Cry like a baby
59. Scottish cap
62. Workplace pay form (2 wds.)
64. Permeate
66. Heidi's home
67. Crystal narcotic, for short
68. Sad sounds
69. Smudge
70. Thumbs-up
71. Third rock from the sun

Down

1. Big name in oil
2. Way out of a car
3. Shrek, for one
4. Dowel
5. Instant
6. Drive too long
7. Short cut
8. Dove's sound
9. Stately trees along the Route
10. Arctic cover (2 wds.)
11. "Excuse me."
12. Covers with pepper spray
13. Leave in, to an editor
19. Missouri attraction, with 34D
22. Paddle
24. Floral necklace on a rearview mirror
26. Where boys will be boys
27. City near Lake Tahoe
28. Distinctive flair
30. Radiant
31. Jesse and Frank James, e.g.
32. Chess piece
34. See 19D
36. Not barefoot
37. Mexican moolah
38. Figure skater's jump
41. London's Big ___
42. Chowed down at White Castle
47. On, as a lamp
48. Least cooked
49. Voters' problem
50. Order's partner
52. Missouri hills brewery
53. Pace
55. Snail trail
56. Knife wound
57. Jerk
58. Phi ___ Kappa
59. Ski lift
60. Backseat relative
61. Work well together
63. Comics shriek
65. Extinct flightless bird

Answers on page 140

Munger Moss Motel at Lebanon, Mo.

Roadside Attractions: Meramec Caverns

Meramec Caverns is one of Missouri's most popular tourist attractions – as evidenced by the 50+ billboards advertising it along Interstate 44 and Route 66. The cavern system is nearly five miles long and was formed from the erosion of large limestock deposits. The mineral formations are amazing – colorful and sparkling. It is just one of more than 6,000 caves in the state, though.

The caverns were discovered by French explorer Philipp Renault in 1720. The Osage Indians had told Renault about the cave they used for shelter in bad weather. Renault named it "Saltpeter Cave," as there was an abundance of saltpeter (potassium nitrate) inside.

The saltpeter mining ended around 1864 when Confederate troops destroyed a Union gunpowder facility inside the cave. Later that century, the cave was bought by Charles Ruepple, who hosted dance parties and live entertainment in the cool cave. In 1933, Ruepple was approached by Lester Benton Dill, who purchased the cave, changed the name, and began offering tours to the public. He explored the cave, even finding another cave and discovering new sections and formations. In 1941, he discovered even more caves and artifacts that turned out to belong to Jesse James.

Since that time, tourists have continued to flock to Meramec's underground world and explore the seven spectacular levels of mineral formations.

Route 66 Sudoku Challenge

Use logic to fill in the boxes so every row, column and 2 x 3 box contain the letters (and numbers) R-O-U-T-E-66. Solutions on page 148.

		66			O
U		T	E		R
O		R	T		U
R			U		

			U	O	66
		66			
	E	T			
			O	E	
			66		
R	66	U			

```
E  E  C  A  W  C  O  N  W  A  Y  V  Z  C  Z
R  O  R  S  M  U  A  N  I  L  P  O  J  L  M
E  S  I  J  T  V  M  S  Q  E  N  E  U  S  P
C  Z  D  Q  I  A  P  W  E  B  B  C  I  T  Y
N  E  A  L  V  S  N  O  N  A  L  P  A  R  S
E  O  L  I  E  C  N  T  Y  N  C  C  K  A  O
P  U  L  S  O  I  G  O  O  O  U  E  E  F  Q
S  L  H  U  T  F  F  K  B  N  B  G  R  F  W
A  B  Q  A  V  N  O  G  O  R  A  D  U  O  O
O  U  S  A  M  P  S  O  N  H  U  P  E  R  U
R  O  L  L  A  E  L  T  T  I  L  O  O  D  S
R  Q  D  O  O  W  K  R  I  K  R  D  B  N  M
Y  G  R  U  B  S  A  E  L  M  T  P  W  Q  D
E  Q  Z  P  A  C  I  F  I  C  H  T  S  I  B
E  O  Y  L  E  B  C  T  L  N  S  S  J  D  I
```

AVILLA	PACIFIC
BOURBON	PLANO
CARTHAGE	POND
CONWAY	ROLLA
CUBA	ROSATI
DOOLITTLE	SAMPSON
EUREKA	SPENCER
JOPLIN	SPRINGFIELD
KIRKWOOD	STANTON
LEASBURG	STRAFFORD
LEBANON	SULLIVAN
NOGO	WEBB CITY

Answers on page 134

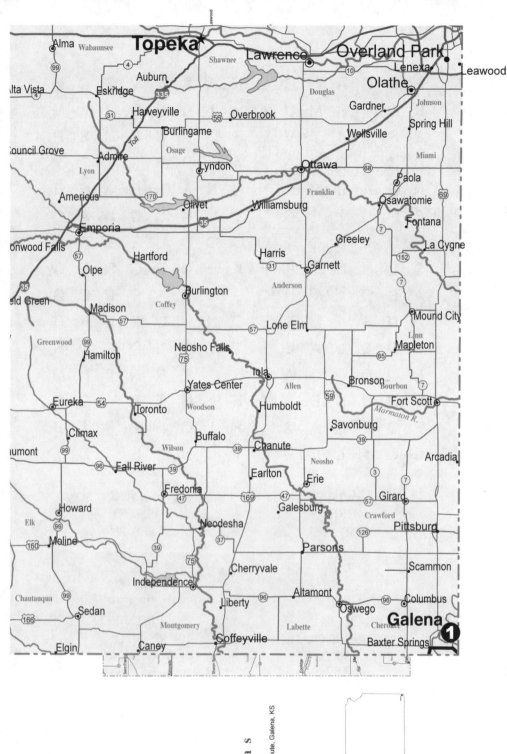

Kansas Landmark:
4 Women on the Route, Galena, KS

K a n s a s

Kansas

While there are just 13.2 miles of Route 66 in Kansas, there are plenty of things to see and do. The Mother Road curves through three towns – Galena, Riverton and Baxter Springs. These towns are steeped with historical buildings that have lived through Kansas' days as a cattle state, mining state and Route 66 hub.

The first town on the Route is Galena, a former mining town. The main attraction is the Howard Litch Historical and Mining Museum. In this old railroad depot building, visitors learn all about Galena and its storied history. Some of the most interesting times came in the early days of Route 66. The road brought prosperity to store keepers, restaurateurs and service station owners in the 1930s. But others in town were hitting hard times – labor strikes led to bloodshed and hundreds of unemployed miners. The lead and zinc started disappearing in the 1970s, the mines closed, and the town's population dwindled to about one tenth of what it was during Galena's heyday.

Phillips 66 Visitors Center at Baxter Springs, Kan.

Another attraction is the Four Women on the Route diner and souvenir store. This is where the International Harvester L-170 truck that inspired the character Mater in the Disney movie *Cars* sits.

Continuing west, the next town on Route 66 is Riverton. The Eisler Brothers

Country Store, built in 1923, is the main remnant of the old road here. This store also had a role in *Cars*. Two miles west is the famous Rainbow Bridge, which crosses Bush Creek. It is a narrow two-lane Marsh arch bridge that is still in use today. The bridge is on the National Register of Historic Places and is the only one of its kind on the Route. Its other claim to fame is that Brad Paisley performed the song "(Get Your Kicks on) Route 66" here for the TLC special "Route 66: Main Street America" in 2000.

Baxter Springs is the last Route 66 town before travelers enter Oklahoma. There are quite a few Route 66-era buildings in the downtown area, including the Heritage Center and Museum. Here visitors learn more about the Mother Road as well as the Civil War and cattle driving times. Baxter Springs was one of the first "cow towns" in Kansas. Thousands of Texas cattle being driven to market in the north stopped here during the journey, and the town constructed corrals for up to 20,000 head of cattle.

A Little Kansas Trivia

1. What was the original title of the movie *Cars*?

2. Where is the truck that was used as the inspiration for one of the characters in *Cars*?

3. Where is the famous Marsh arch bridge?

4. What is Kansas' state nickname?

5. What is the slogan on Kansas' buffalo personalized license plates?

6. Which metal is processed in the Galena smelter?

Answers on page 155

Unscramble

Unscramble these letters to form a word or words related to Route 66 in Kansas. Answers on page 154.

AAEGLN   _____

EEIMPR CIYT   _____

AETRXB SSPRGIN   _____

AODS FAINTNUO   _____

OOTRM NIN   _____

ONVCERBITEL   _____

Route 66 Soda Fountain at Baxter Springs, Kan.

Route 66 Sudoku Challenge

Use logic to fill in the boxes so every row, column and 2 x 3 box contain the letters (and numbers) R-O-U-T-E-66. Solutions on page 149.

		O			66
O		R	66		T
T		66	O		U
E			R		

		T	U	66	
	O				
			R		
		U			
				O	
	66	O	T		

```
B  S  I  D  I  L  I  Q  C  A  O  M  C  O  D
P  T  K  Y  A  K  E  E  R  C  L  A  O  H  S
X  J  D  C  J  O  X  T  W  Y  F  P  S  H  A
M  P  B  E  N  A  R  I  V  E  R  T  O  N  T
A  T  Y  R  O  U  T  E  N  D  Y  R  D  U  U
O  S  G  N  I  R  P  S  R  E  T  X  A  B  R
C  O  P  L  T  D  R  E  X  C  I  Y  F  O  M
A  P  A  O  A  M  G  E  R  A  C  A  O  S  K
X  N  V  I  T  V  U  E  H  R  E  W  U  I  M
E  G  E  Z  S  S  E  S  Q  S  R  H  N  I  N
T  I  M  L  S  K  T  D  E  Y  I  G  T  Q  H
A  S  E  R  A  H  K  S  I  U  P  I  A  U  E
H  V  N  F  G  G  E  B  E  N  M  H  I  J  J
C  I  T  N  U  L  B  L  V  R  E  C  N  C  B
V  P  Q  Y  W  Q  I  I  L  F  Z  R  W  I  O
```

BAXTER SPRINGS	MUSEUM
BLUNT	PAVEMENT
BRIDGE	REST STOP
CAFE	RIVERTON
CARS	ROAD
CHAT	ROUTE
DINER	SHELL
EMPIRE CITY	SHOAL CREEK
GALENA	SHORT CREEK
GAS STATION	SIGN POST
HIGHWAY	SODA FOUNTAIN
LANE	TEXACO

Answers on page 134

1	2	3	4		5	6	7	8		9	10	11	12	13
14					15					16				
17					18					19				
20				21				22	23					
24				25					26					
		27				28	29				30	31	32	
33	34	35				36				37				
38						39				40				
41					42				43					
44				45				46						
		47				48				49	50	51		
52	53	54			55		56			57				
58					59	60				61				
62					63					64				
65					66					67				

Across

1. Catholic service
5. Present
9. Blunder
14. Fencing blade
15. Lot size
16. ___ Island National Monument
17. Burn a bit
18. Pride member
19. Shades of blue
20. South Carolina military school
22. Aggravation
24. Want ___
25. "___ questions?"
26. QB's cry
27. Modern courtroom evidence
28. Legal paper
30. Absorb, with "up"
33. Sight-related
36. In a bit
37. Bishop of Rome
38. Stallone's "Rocky" co-star
39. BBs, e.g.
40. Cereal grasses
41. Highway division
42. Kind of school
43. Baby grand, e.g.
44. Giant slugger Mel
45. Enlist in
46. Pester

47. Phillips 66 product
48. Sunbather's goal
49. A colorful fish
52. Comes from behind
56. No longer around
58. Thread holder
59. Fruity pastry
61. Memo
62. Liveliness
63. Basilica area
64. Flim-___
65. Inquisitive sort
66. Bar order
67. Former GM brand

Down

1. Muhammad's birthplace
2. Orchard pest
3. Does an usher's job
4. Blood fluids
5. City named for the lead ore found there
6. Coldly
7. To and ___
8. Motel room alternative
9. Leave the car (2 wds.)
10. Alaskan native
11. Spare tire?
12. "___ 'er up!"
13. Latin 101 verb
21. Do the jig

23. Zoo heavyweight
27. In ___ straits
28. 4 ___ on the Route
29. Frolic
30. Bean used to make miso
31. Sign in a souvenir shop window
32. 100 centavos
33. Norse capital
34. First-rate, slangily
35. Windshield option
36. Delhi wrap
37. Bluenose
42. Sit for a photo
43. Fourth down play
45. Key employee?
46. ___ Springs, home of Hangman's Elm
47. Shortstop's equipment
48. To the point
49. Small hill
50. Group of eight
51. Agenda entries
52. Invitation letters
53. Impersonator
54. Colorful Australian parrot
55. Wild guess
57. Road trip data
60. *Tarzan* extra

Answers on page 141

Roadside Attractions: Cars in Real Life

Route 66 came to life in the 2006 Disney/Pixar movie *Cars*. And so did the International Harvester L-170 truck that sits outside the Four Women on the Route diner and souvenir store in Galena. This truck inspired the character Mater (voiced by Larry the Cable Guy).

The animated film's setting was a world of anthropomorphic cars and other vehicles with eyes on their windshields. Other characters were voiced by Paul Newman, Owen Wilson, Bonnie Hunt and George Carlin.

Route 66 inspired the movie. Directors John Lasseter and Joe Ranft and their crew traveled the Route, and although the names have changed, travelers will notice some of the Mother Road's most popular landmarks in the movie. Among these are:

* The Cozy Cone Motel, which was based on the wigwam motels along the Route and named after the Cozy Dog Drive-In in Springfield, Illinois.

* Ramone's House of Body Art resembles the art deco U-Drop Inn in Shamrock, Texas.

* Lizzie's Curio Shop has a "Here It Is" sign, inspired by the many Jack Rabbit Trading Post billboards throughout Arizona.

In the story, the stock-car racing season ends in a tie between a legend (Strip "The King" Weathers), a bad guy (Chick Hicks) and a cocky rookie (Lightning McQueen). The tiebreaker race is scheduled in California, and the three cars separately make their way across the country. McQueen runs into some

bad luck in Radiator Springs and ends up doing community service repaving a road. McQueen learns Radiator Springs was once a popular stop on Route 66 but was bypassed by the interstate, leaving many businesses abandoned. McQueen makes some friends (including a former racing star), touches a few hearts, and leaves town for the race. After the race (which Chick dubiously won), McQueen moves his racing team to Radiator Springs, revitalizing the town.

The film was nominated for two Academy Awards. It won the Golden Globe Award for Best Animated Feature Film and is due for a sequel in 2011.

```
 1     2     3     4     5     6     7
 8                 9
 10              11
 12              13
 14       15     16  17         18
              19
 20  21      22      23  24
 25          26
 27              28
```

Across

8. Chevy brand
9. Came after
10. Pretend to sing
11. Home to 4 Women on the Route
12. Kleenex paper
13. Car rental company
14. Opposed to
16. Retro design style, popular on the Route (2 wds.)
20. Kansas' neighbor
23. Stockings
25. Route city: ___ Springs
26. Major roads
27. Visitor center locale (2 wds.)
28. Washington bill

Down

1. Refereeing a baseball game
2. Sunflower State
3. Washes clothes
4. Type of remark
5. Scheduled plane trip
6. Turnpike (2 wds.)
7. Muscle rupture protusion
15. Bother
17. Deserter
18. Snickers, e.g. (2 wds.)
19. Drive-in waitresses
21. Pencil end
22. Walks with a swagger
24. Route lake in Kansas

Answers on page 141

Oklahoma

Oklahoma is proud of its Route 66 heritage. That fact is evident as visitors travel the road's 400 miles across the state. The Route has been well preserved. In fact, Oklahoma has more original Route 66 road than any other state. Travelers can stay on it through almost the entire state, though there are a few points where one must briefly merge onto the highway.

Route 66 was born in Oklahoma, the brainchild of Cyrus Avery. Avery owned a service station and restaurant in Tulsa and became Oklahoma's first highway commissioner. He led the committee that created the U.S. highway system in 1926, proposed the road linking Chicago to L.A., and even gave it the name "66."

It's no surprise, then, that Oklahoma was the first state to install historic markers along Route 66, the first to have

The Blue Whale at Catoosa, Okla.

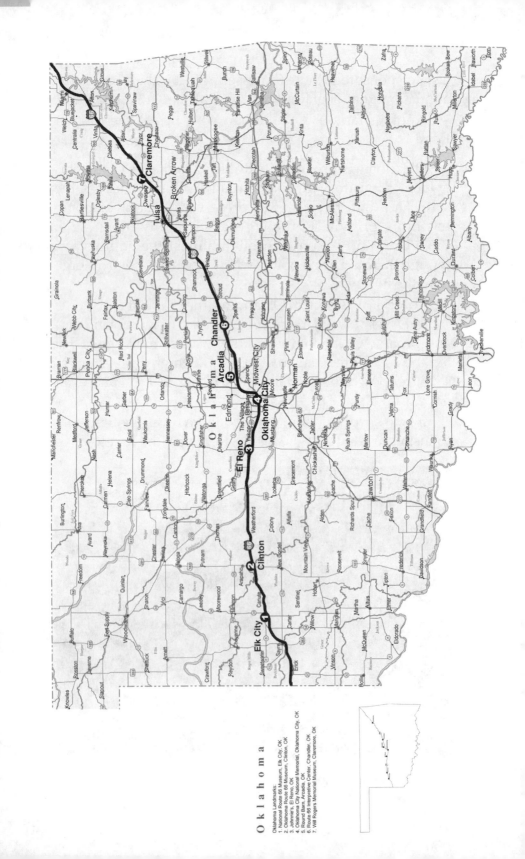

Oklahoma

Oklahoma Landmarks:
1. National Route 66 Museum, Elk City, OK
2. Oklahoma Route 66 Museum, Clinton, OK
3. Johnnie's, El Reno, OK
4. Oklahoma City National Memorial, Oklahoma City, OK
5. Round Barn Arcadia, OK
6. Route 66 Interpretive Center, Chandler, OK
7. Will Rogers Memorial Museum, Claremore, OK

a state-sponsored Route 66 museum and is the home to the annual International Route 66 Festival held in Tulsa in June.

Another famous Oklahoman with ties to the Mother Road is Will Rogers. This humorist and writer, born near Claremore, was in 70+ movies and wrote more than 4,000 national newspaper columns. In fact, Route 66 is often called the Will Rogers Highway.

Heading west, one of the state's first attractions – the Coleman Theatre – is in Miami. This theatre, dating back to 1927, was built by mining millionaire George L. Coleman, who hoped to bring culture to town. And that he did. The theatre hosted vaudeville shows and movies. Stars like Will Rogers, the Three Stooges and Tom Mix appeared at the theatre, which is now owned by the city and houses Route 66 memorabilia.

Further west in Claremore is the Will Rogers Memorial. This museum features all kinds of Rogers memorabilia, documents and photographs. There is also a theater that shows his movies and speeches. Rogers' tomb is on the 20-acre grounds.

No Route 66 trip would be complete without a stop in Catoosa and a visit to the Blue Whale park. Though the park is now closed, the Blue Whale swimming hole is one of the most recognizable attractions on the Route. The Blue Whale was built on a pond by Hugh Davis in the early 1970s. He built it as a gift to his wife Zelda, who collected all things whale. While it started out as a family swimming area, locals and travelers showed interest, encouraging Davis to open the bright blue attraction to the public.

In Tulsa, travelers will see historic buildings. One of these is the Rose Bowl, a landmark dome-shaped building that has been a bowling alley and hangout since the 1950s. One of the most visited Route 66 sites in town is the Vickery Phillips 66 station. The building has been restored and is now an Avis rental car location. There are several examples of 1920s and 1930s art deco buildings in town, and visitors may want to take a walking tour of these gems. The 11th

Street Bridge – renamed the Cyrus Avery Route 66 Memorial Bridge in 2004 – is just one example.

Right before entering Oklahoma City, travelers often stop at Arcadia, home to the Round Barn. Constructed in 1898, the barn formerly housed livestock, but today it hosts special events, like weddings. The barn is 45 feet tall and 60 feet in diameter. The builder, W.H. Odor, reportedly built the barn in a circular shape to help it withstand tornados.

Sweet T's Antique Store/Soda Pop store is another popular attraction in Arcadia. Its claim to fame is the world's largest (60-foot tall) soda pop bottle that resides in the front of the building. The gas station/mini-mart/restaurant has hundreds of pop bottles as its décor and sells at least 400 varieties of soda. It is a newcomer to Route 66, but many thirsty travelers find it a worthy stop.

Route 66 runs through the state capital of Oklahoma City, home to one of the world's top livestock markets. Here, visitors often stop by the Oklahoma City National Memorial and Museum. This stark memorial not only pays tribute to the 168 people killed when Timothy McVeigh set off a bomb in front of the Murrah building in 1995, but also to victims of all terrorist attacks. It features two gates, a reflecting pool and a field of 168 empty chairs. Also on the grounds is the Survivor Tree, an elm that withstood the explosions and is now a symbol of courage.

West of Oklahoma City are Clinton and Elk City, both of which have popular Route 66 museums. The Clinton museum is the first official state-operated Route 66 museum in the country. Opened in 1968 as the Museum of the Western Trails, it changed its focus to the Mother Road in 1995. Exhibits feature treasures from all along the Route. Visitors can get a feel for what the road was like during various times in U.S. history, experiencing the vehicles, music, restaurants, lodging and attractions all in one building. The Elk City National Route 66 Museum focuses more on the people who worked, traveled and lived on Route 66. There are displays from all eight states along the

Oklahoma City National Memorial

road. When in Elk City, visitors sometimes make a stop at Parker Rig 114, which – at 179 feet – is the world's tallest nonworking oil rig.

A Little Oklahoma Trivia

Match these celebrities with their Oklahoma hometowns:

1. Country Western singer Garth Brooks
2. Newsman Paul Harvey
3. Baseball star Mickey Mantle
4. Singer Roger Miller
5. Humorist Will Rogers
6. Astronaut Tom Stafford

a. Claremore
b. Commerce
c. Erick
d. Tulsa
e. Weatherford
f. Yukon

Answers on page 141

Milk Bottle Building at Oklahoma City, Okla.

Route 66 Sudoku Challenge

Use logic to fill in the boxes so every row, column and 2 x 3 box contain the letters (and numbers) R-O-U-T-E-66. Solutions on page 149-150.

			U		66
		66	E		
U		R			
			O		U
		U	R		
O		E			

T	R				U
				E	
					T
66					
	E				
U				R	E

Quote Box

Start at the T in the 6th column of the 6th row and work your way up, down, left or right (not diagonally) to spell out the message on the wall of the building in Texola, Okla. Solution on page 158.

N	Y	W	H	E	R	E	N	E
A	E	P	S	I	H	T	R	A
A	C	L	A	C	E	S	O	T
L	T	E	C	A	E	P	L	H
P	H	K	E	L	H	T	A	I
S	I	I	L	P	**T**	E	C	S
O	T	H	E	R	H	B	E	M
O	N	S	E	R	E	T	S	U

```
S  W  S  Z  A  O  T  G  D  Z  G  U  W  C  N
T  E  T  M  G  U  E  H  N  F  Z  E  H  O  I
R  E  L  D  N  A  H  C  O  J  P  E  T  H  T
O  L  N  K  R  X  B  S  M  E  L  N  Y  A  L
U  O  I  Y  C  L  W  D  D  S  I  D  V  X  J
D  L  P  Y  S  I  O  I  E  L  R  K  O  H  W
S  S  A  S  O  O  T  A  C  O  C  C  D  A  L
W  F  A  O  W  F  S  Y  N  I  W  I  P  G  A
F  S  L  P  W  A  I  E  R  I  M  A  I  M  Z
R  N  O  K  U  Y  R  E  H  T  U  L  S  A  D
X  N  X  D  J  L  B  W  G  Q  O  T  P  E  P
A  C  E  O  E  I  P  V  I  N  I  T  A  Z  O
A  F  T  O  N  S  T  A  B  C  S  N  B  H  E
E  Q  J  T  Q  K  W  C  V  U  K  U  R  O  T
N  Y  Z  U  S  P  K  C  Y  A  A  R  B  F  I
```

AFTON	GEARY
BRISTOW	HYDRO
CATOOSA	LUTHER
CHANDLER	MIAMI
CHELSEA	QUAPAW
CLINTON	SAPULPA
DEPEW	STROUD
EDMOND	TEXOLA
EL RENO	TULSA
ELK CITY	VINITA
ERICK	WARWICK
FOYIL	YUKON

Answers on page 135

1	2	3		4	5	6	7	8		9	10	11	12	13
14				15						16				
17				18						19				
20			21				22	23			24			
25				26		27				28				
		29			30			31			32	33	34
35	36	37								38				
39				40			41	42			43			
44		45	46			47			48	49				
50				51		52						56	57	58
		53			54			55						
59	60	61		62					63					
64			65		66	67	68	69			70			
71					72						73			
74					75						76			

Across

1. By way of
4. Red Cross supply
9. Hooded snake
14. ___ and outs
15. Poet's Muse
16. Part of "the works"
17. Tit for ___
18. Spoke Persian?
19. Audacity
20. Excuse
22. Type widths
24. Morning moisture
25. Home of the Onion Burger (2 wds.)
27. Influence

29. Place for a boutonniere
31. Sarah Palin's state
35. Tulsa deli order
38. Not bold
39. Lennon's lady
40. Searches for the original route
43. Be in debt
44. Yucatán natives
47. Enjoying the roadside scenery (2 wds.)
50. See 4A
52. Like the drinks in the cooler in your trunk (2 wds.)
53. Austrian composer
55. Oklahoma city closest to Texas

59. Not even
62. Observe
63. Play a banjo
64. Diner pie filler, often
66. Percolate
70. Back then
71. Excessive
72. Indy 500 winner Castroneves
73. Half a score
74. Fab Four drummer
75. Acquired relative
76. Unit of work

Down

1. Aqua ___
2. 2,448 miles on the Route (2 wds.)
3. Moving about
4. Business conference
5. Poet's preposition
6. Uncooked
7. Western Indian
8. Ford's T
9. Advise on the best road to take
10. Small bill
11. Wren or hen
12. Wander the Route
13. All over again
21. Car strap: seat ___
23. Extinct flightless bird

26. Brilliantly colored fish
27. Home to the Oklahoma Route 66 Museum
28. Mai ___
30. Relative of an ostrich
32. Oklahoma City haze
33. New Zealander on the Route
34. Mideast's Gulf of ___
35. Ceremonial splendor
36. ___ retentive
37. Kind of bean
41. *The Joy Luck Club* author
42. Burlesque bit
45. Bat wood
46. Pulverizer
48. Rink entertainment (2 wds.)
49. Waiting room call
51. Sailor's affirmative
54. Indian metropolis
56. Speak from a soapbox
57. Winter Olympian
58. In the midst of
59. Numbered composition
60. Fender blemish
61. Arp's art
65. Mongrel
67. Bard's nightfall
68. Pledge of Allegiance ender
69. Cloak-and-dagger org.

Answers on page 142

Roadside Attractions: Will Rogers

Will Rogers is Oklahoma's most famous son. Born in Oologah (near Claremore) in 1879, Rogers was a Cherokee-American cowboy, actor and humorist. He made 71 movies and wrote thousands of newspaper columns, many of which are on view at the Will Rogers Memorial in Claremore. At the time of his death in an Alaska airplane crash (1935), Rogers was the highest-paid actor in Hollywood.

Rogers also led an interesting life prior to entering the entertainment industry. He tried to work as a gaucho in Argentina and a horse trainer for the British Army. He also spent some time in South Africa and Australia and at several ranches in the United States. He began his show biz career in "Texas Jack's Wild West Circus." He worked as the circus' trick roper.

Rogers got his start in vaudeville when he was a patron at a Madison Square Garden event. A wild steer ventured into the stands, where Rogers immediately roped it. This landed him on the front page of the *New York Times* and, later, as a star in New York. In 1915, Rogers started a stint in Florenz Ziegfeld's "Midnight Frolic." He delivered monologues, beginning each evening with his trademark line, "All I know is what I read in the papers." He moved on to the Ziegfeld Follies, silent films and, finally, "talkies," becoming one of the biggest stars of the 1920s and 1930s.

He began a writing career, went on a lecture tour, and hosted the Academy Awards. Rogers' statue is one of two representing the state of Oklahoma in

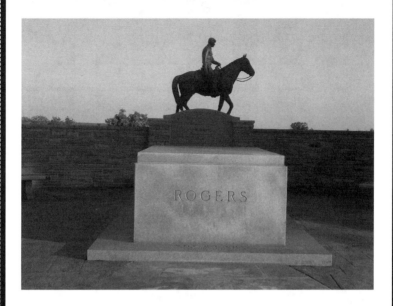

the United States Capitol building. Legend has it that each president rubs the statue's foot for good luck on the way to the State of the Union Address.

In Oklahoma, Route 66 travelers can go to Rogers' birthplace in Oologah and the Will Rogers Memorial Museum in Claremore.

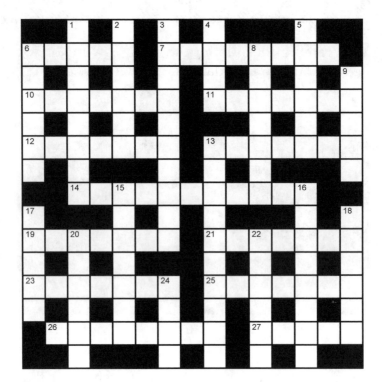

Across

6. Ellipses
7. Dutiful
10. Home of the National Route 66 Museum (2 wds.)
11. Walden Pond author
12. Lookout man
13. Customers
14. Old fashioned writing table with a sliding cover (2 wds.)
19. Previously owned vehicle (2 wds.)
21. Radioactive element
23. Fertilizer-free food
25. Oklahoma Route 66 museum site
26. Will Rogers' is Claremore, e.g.
27. Bee and Jemima

Down

1. Rear entrance
2. Souvenir shop purchase
3. Ad agency employee
4. Exam
5. Monica Lewinsky, e.g.
6. Ultimatum words (2 wds.)
8. Worship
9. Home to "Father of Route 66" Cyrus Avery
13. Starbucks order
15. Driver's permit
16. Weaving a sweater by hand
17. Garth Brooks' hometown
18. Makes better
20. Yuletide drink
22. Not a vegetable or mineral
24. Large black bird

Answers on page 142

Unscramble

Unscramble these letters to form a word or words related to Route 66 in Oklahoma. Answers on page154.

LIWL SERGOR   _____

SAULT   _____

UEBL WHAEL   _____

AAESB TTSAOIN   _____

OOINN RREGBU   _____

RRAHUM IILDNGUB   _____

The Round Barn in Arcadia

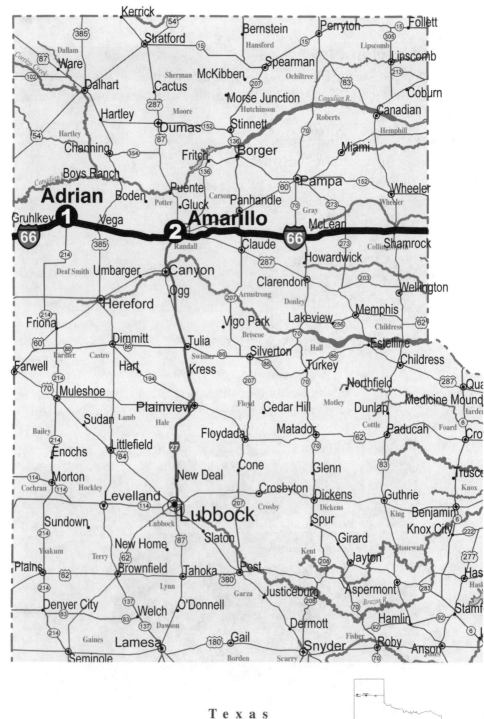

Texas

Texas Landmarks:
1. Midpoint Cafe, A drian, TX
2. The Big Texan, Amarillo, TX

Texas

Texas may have the second-smallest Route 66 path, but it certainly does not lack interesting sites.

U-Drop Inn at Shamrock, Tex.

One of the first Texan towns travelers hit is Shamrock. This small town is home to the U-Drop Inn. This art deco masterpiece was built in 1936 and once housed a service station on one side and a restaurant on the other. The newly restored building now hosts the Shamrock Chamber of Commerce, a gift shop and a visitor's center. The building served as a model for Ramone's body shop in the movie *Cars*.

About 20 miles west of Shamrock is McLean. One of the most unique museums on the Route – the Devil's Rope Barbed Wire Museum – is located here. This museum documents the history of barbed wire, tools and other devices used in fence construction and maintenance. It has thousands of varieties of barbed wire. As with most museums on the Route, it also has some displays on the history of Route 66 (and the headquarters of the Texas Historic Route 66 Association is located here). A few blocks down the road is the first Phillips 66 gas station in Texas, opened in 1927. Though travelers can no longer fill their tanks at the station, they can get a glimpse of what a service station looked like in the 1930s – 19 cent gasoline and all!

Visitors entering Groom, a town with 500 residents, are greeted by an unusual water tower calling the area "Britten, USA." This leaning water tower was built off-kilter to draw attention to the once busy Britten Truck Stop, Garage and Restaurant. The business is gone, but the tower remains, a must-see on any Route 66 trip. On the west side of Groom is the tallest cross in the Western Hemisphere. The Cross of our Lord Jesus Christ Ministries is 190-feet tall and can be seen from a distance of 20 miles away on clear days.

Around Amarillo, travelers pass cattle ranches that look much the same as they did in the 1800s. Amarillo was the heart of the Old West, and there is still some evidence of that today. The original Route 66 alignment hits Sixth Street, which has numerous old buildings that are now restaurants, boutiques and antique stores. The Nat Dine and Dance Palace once featured big bands in the 1940s and rock 'n' roll in the 1950s. Today it is a haunted bookstore.

The Big Texan is one of the most popular stops in Amarillo. Built in 1960, this true western steak house promises a free 72-ounce steak to anyone who can eat it in an hour or less. This successful promotion has drawn visitors in for 50 years, and just one in six people actually finishes. (The rest end up paying $50 for their meal.)

Cadillac Ranch near Amarillo, Tex.

Sign at the MidPoint Café in Adrian, Tex.

Amarillo's Cadillac Ranch is perhaps the most iconic of all attractions on the Mother Road. Ten Cadillacs (1948 to 1963 models) are buried hood down in a wheat field just west of the city. Built by Texas millionaire Stanley Marsh III in 1973, the Cadillac Ranch is an artistic endeavor like no other. Visitors bearing their own spray paint can stop here and create some vehicle art of their own.

The final stop in Texas is the tiny town of Adrian. Home to just 150 residents and 12 businesses, Adrian's claim to fame is that it is at the midway point of Route 66. The MidPoint Café, constructed in 1928, has been a restaurant since the Route began. What started out as a one-room eatery with a dirt floor is now the longest continually operating restaurant on Route 66. While its homestyle cooking shouldn't be missed, the MidPoint Café is also worth a look because of its Route 66 memorabilia collection.

Route 66 Sudoku Challenge

Use logic to fill in the boxes so every row, column and 2 x 3 box contain the letters (and numbers) R-O-U-T-E-66. Solutions on page 150.

				U	
			O	66	
		O	R		
		T	U		
	E	66			
	O				

			66	E	
		T		R	
		O	U		
		66	T		
	U		E		
	O	E			

Roadside Attractions: The Big Texan

The Big Texan in Amarillo is famous for its big steaks. The promise of a free 72-ounce steak to anyone who can eat it in an hour or less draws in half a million travelers off Route 66 each year.

Bob Lee opened the Big Texas Steak Ranch in 1960. Cowboys from area ranches came to the Big Texan with huge appetites. Legend has it that the promotion started one day when a particularly hungry cowboy came in and said he could "eat the whole, darned cow." Bob took (and lost) that bet and a tradition was born.

But the Big Texan offers more than 72-ounce steaks, t-shirts and a certificate of achievement. It has steak and eggs, a breakfast buffet, free meals on your birthday, fried rattlesnake, fried mountain oysters and the Big Texan Singers. There's a gift shop inside and a sister motel next door. The motel looks like an Old West town's main street and features a Texas-shaped swimming pool. There's even a horse hotel with 20 stalls where today's cowboys can leave their animals while they dine.

The restaurant's Web site features a list of all winning contestants and has a live camera focused on patrons chowing down. The quickest victory was in 2008, when Joey Chestnut ate the piece of beef in 8 minutes and 52 seconds.

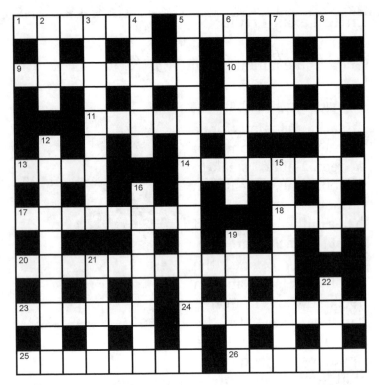

Across

1. MidPoint Café site
5. Drive with no time to spare (3 _____ wds.)
9. Aped
10. Fly a plane
11. Office greeter
13. Surrealist Spanish painter
14. Not now (2 wds.)
17. Stick-in-the-mud driver
18. Motel room cleaner
20. 30-minute TV ads
23. Sticky note brand
24. Camouflage
25. Alice in Wonderland event (2 _____ wds.)
26. Devil's Rope Museum town

Down

2. Roosevelt coin
3. Rice novel: ___ *with the Vampire*
4. Observe
5. Fourth of July
6. Site of The Big Texan restaurant
7. Workers' group
8. Broiler with a rotating spit
12. Move beyond liking someone _____ (3 wds.)
15. Knucklehead
16. Texas' nickname: The ___ State
19. Kidnapper's demand
21. How beer is often served (2 wds.)
22. Singapore's continent

Answers on page 143

A Little Texas Trivia

1. Where is the famous U-DROP INN?

2. What is "devil's rope"?

3. Which city is home to the world's largest cross?

4. What is the western-most city in Texas on Route 66?

5. Who founded The Big Texan restaurant?

6. How many ounces is The Big Texan's "free" steak?

Answers on page 156

Unscramble

Unscramble these letters to form a word or words related to Route 66 in Texas. Answers on page 154.

HET GIB NAXET   _____

LLAADICC CHARN   _____

AALLMRIO   _____

TERWA WERTO   _____

MIDTPOIN FEAC   _____

OOWBYC   _____

Across

1. Worry about finding a rest stop
5. El ___, Tex.
9. Like construction zone traffic
14. Running behind
15. ___ *Karenina*
16. Ball girl
17. Previously unknown (2 wds.)
19. Indoor rodeo venue
20. Asian capital
21. 72-oz. steak place, with "The" (2 wds.)
23. Catches sight of
26. Take to court
27. A plant disease
29. "___ does it!"
33. "The Yellow Rose of Texas" city
37. Winter road problem: pot___
38. Cotton bundle
39. "As ___ as a judge"
42. Store sign
43. Columnist Bombeck
44. Texas city that shares a name with the voice of Fred Flintstone (2 wds.)
46. Drop from the eye
47. Modernize the road signs
49. Neighbor of Wash.
50. Las Vegas home

54. Amarillo-area ranch subject
59. Swelling
61. Keep after
62. The top number of a fraction
65. Related on the mother's side
66. Russia's ___ Mountains
67. Lady's escort
68. Criminal
69. School session
70. Work units

Down

1. Bugs
2. Rajah's wife
3. Spirit of a people
4. Get ready to drive? (2 wds.)
5. Golfer's goal
6. What's more
7. Nose-in-the-air type driver
8. Loutish
9. Lessen
10. "The Way We ___"
11. Bend, as a muscle
12. Forearm bone
13. React to a sharp turn
18. Excuse
22. Kind of feeling
24. Building additions

25. Farm storage cylinder
28. Spoil (2 wds.)
29. Norse thunder god
30. Bill Clinton's Arkansas birthplace
31. On the safe side, at sea
32. Care for
33. Aid in crime
34. Foal's mother
35. ___ mater
36. Backside of the car
40. Distinctive flair
41. Miles per hour, e.g.
45. "When pigs fly!"
47. WWW address
48. Oil source
49. Antiquated
51. Words of wisdom
52. Discourage
53. Honor ___ thieves
54. Restaurant cook
55. Five-star
56. Twofold
57. Passionate about
58. Medical breakthrough
60. Liberal pursuits
63. Fold, spindle or mutilate
64. Route's shade tree

Answers on page 143

```
E  R  C  H  E  E  S  E  B  U  R  G  E  R  S
T  L  O  N  G  H  O  R  N  U  I  B  F  C  H
C  C  V  T  H  E  B  I  G  T  E  X  A  N  A
B  G  U  M  R  A  F  G  U  B  C  D  C  N  M
C  O  I  R  N  E  L  G  A  Z  I  D  T  I  R
O  V  E  G  A  M  A  R  I  L  L  O  N  S  O
N  E  T  T  I  R  B  E  L  D  U  Z  I  U  C
W  F  S  V  G  E  I  A  S  E  L  U  O  T  K
A  M  U  T  D  P  C  S  D  E  D  S  P  C  V
Y  A  C  W  E  R  J  Y  M  R  T  G  D  A  N
E  F  I  L  A  A  O  S  O  N  I  V  I  C  V
V  R  P  N  E  B  K  P  O  A  J  A  M  T  W
E  P  C  E  W  A  I  O  R  L  F  A  N  O  B
A  H  T  O  Y  N  N  O  G  A  J  R  Z  A  X
X  E  C  P  N  L  O  N  E  S  T  A  R  L  D
```

ADRIAN	GLENRIO
ALANREED	GREASY SPOON
AMARILLO	GROOM
APPLE PIE	LONESTAR
BARBED WIRE	LONGHORN
BRITTEN	MCLEAN
BUG FARM	MIDPOINT CAFE
CACTUS INN	SHAMROCK
CADILLAC RANCH	STEAK
CHEESEBURGER	THE BIG TEXAN
CONWAY	U DROP INN
COWBOY	VEGA

Answers on page 135

New Mexico

The New Mexico stretch of Route 66 is one of great variety. The road goes through the state's largest cities and tourist attractions (Albuquerque, Gallup) as well as wide open western landscapes. With its colorful mesas, Indian heritage and great beauty, it's a state that keeps travelers interested and wondering what is just around the bend.

Modern Route 66 sculpture at Tucumcari, N.M.

One of the first towns travelers hit in New Mexico is Tucumcari. By the late 1960s, most of the state's Route 66 had been replaced by I-40, except the first 40 miles from Glenrio to Tucumcari. Here it was a narrow two-lane highway, which became known as Slaughter Lane because of the high number of accidents and fatalities on the road. Because of this, I-40 finally came to town in 1981.

In Tucumcari, the sculpture in front of the convention center is a must-see. This chrome '66 tailfin is one of the most modern pieces of Route 66 art on the Mother Road. Tucumcari's southwestern pride is on display all around town, where there are 17 large murals on various buildings. The Tucumcari Historical Museum has a nice collection of Route 66 memorabilia. One of the best-known sites in town is the Blue Swallow Motel. This 1939 motel on the National Register of Historic Places is unique in that visitors get not only a hotel room but a drive-in garage for their car – just like at home!

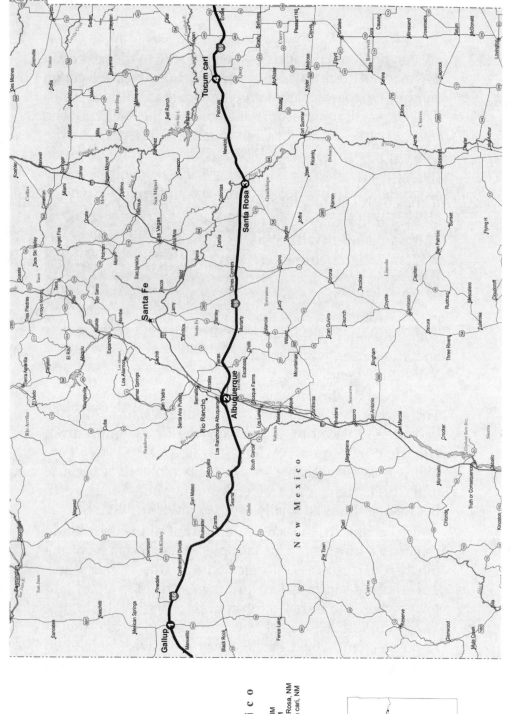

New Mexico

New Mexico Landmarks:
1. El Rancho Motel, Gallup, NM
2. 66 Diner, Alburquerque, NM
3. Joseph's Bar & Grill, Santa Rosa, NM
4. Blue Swallow Motel, Tucum cari, NM

As the Route parallels I-40 on the way to the next main town, Santa Rosa, travelers see many vintage service station pumps, billboards painted on large rocks and stone ruins. Travelers will notice iconic billboards of the Fat Man, who once advertised the old Club Café (now Joseph's), before driving into town. In Santa Rosa, visitors chow down on quesadillas at Joseph's Bar and Grill and examine the classic Corvettes and Thunderbirds at Bozo and Anna's Route 66 Auto Museum.

Route 66 runs through the center of Albuquerque. The downtown area is specked with classic buildings, including old theaters, hotels and restaurants, in Art Deco and Pueblo Deco styles. One of the most spectacular landmarks is the KiMo Theater, built in 1927. The state's largest city, Albuquerque is also known as the Ballooning Capital of the World. This is due to the International Balloon Fiesta, an October event that hosts 700+ balloons and attracts thousands of spectators each year.

From Albuquerque to Gallup, Route 66 travelers venture upon old bridges, including the Parker Through Truss Bridge that cross the Rio Puerco (just west of Albuquerque) and the Parker Pony Truss Bridge in Correo. There are old trading posts and service stations (some in ruins) in Correo, Budville, Cubero and San Fidel that travelers can visit before stopping at Grants.

A town of nearly 9,000 residents, Grants is remembered for the uranium boom that lasted from the 1950s to 1980s. The Grants Mining Museum is right on Route 66, surrounded by the beauty of high desert country. Grants has several historic buildings on Route 66, including the Grants Café, the West Theater, the Zia Motel, the Uranium Café, the Lux Theater and the Monte Carlo Restaurant.

The western path to Gallup is full of mountains, lava fields (badlands) and old uranium mines. The road goes through the Continental Divide just past Thoreau and hits Route 66's highest point in New Mexico at Top O' the World.

Rehoboth is home to the Red Rocks that appeared in John Ford's 1940 film, *The Grapes of Wrath*.

Gallup is the main stop before travelers come to Arizona. Often called the "Indian Capital of the World," Gallup is in the heart of Navajo, Hopi and Zuni lands. There are quite a few art galleries and trading posts where travelers can shop for Indian trinkets. The turquoise jewelry is some of the best in the world. Many Hollywood Westerns were filmed in Gallup in the 1940s and 1950s, and the El Rancho Hotel – where many movie stars stayed – is a must-see.

A Little New Mexico Trivia

1. Where on Route 66 is the only service station to have operated continuously from the Route's origin to the present?

2. Because of re-routing of the original route, in which city can you actually stand at the intersection of Route 66 and Route 66?

3. Which famous Tucumcari motel is named after a colorful bird?

4. Which university does Route 66 pass through in Albuquerque?

5. In which city has "The Fat Man" achieved celebrity status?

6. Which two U.S. presidents stayed at the El Rancho in Gallup?

Answers on page 156

Unscramble

Unscramble these letters to form a word or words related to Route 66 in New Mexico. Answers on page 154.

CCUUMARIT   _____

AANTS AROS   _____

RQQUUUEELBA   _____

TFA AMN   _____

ACELNRT AEENUV   _____

ALLGUP   _____

Aztec Motel at Albuquerque, N.M.

Roadside Attractions: El Rancho Hotel

In the 1950s and 1960s, the famous El Rancho Hotel in Gallup hosted movie stars like John Wayne, Ronald Reagan, Spencer Tracy, Katharine Hepburn and Humphrey Bogart. Today's visitors can see their autographed photos on the walls and even sleep in star-themed (and named) rooms.

The hotel was built in 1936 for R.E. Griffith, the brother of movie director D.W. Griffith. Many Westerns were filmed in Gallup, so the actors, directors and film crews always stayed there. The El Rancho was known for its outstanding service and rooms, and its staff was trained by the Fred Harvey Company.

The hotel attracts attention right away. The three-story brick building has white wooden trim and promises "Charm of Yesterday, Convenience of Tomorrow." As visitors enter the hotel, they see the main lobby that has the feel of a hunting lodge in the Wild West. It is furnished with dark wood pieces, Navajo rugs and deer heads. There's a huge fireplace and a wooden staircase that leads to the balcony overlooking the lobby.

The hotel El Rancho was listed in the National Register of Historic Places in 1988.

Route 66 Sudoku Challenge

Use logic to fill in the boxes so every row, column and 2 x 3 box contain the letters (and numbers) R-O-U-T-E-66. Solutions on page 151.

				O	66
R				T	
66					R
U					E
	E				O
O	U				

		T	R	U	
			66	O	
		R	O		
		O	U		
	T	66			
	O	E	T		

Across

1. Not "fer"
5. Gush from a hot radiator
9. Coarse file
13. Driving in the wrong lane
14. New Mexico's Four Corners neighbor
15. Free-for-all
16. Home of the Blue Swallow Motel
18. Birdlike
19. Kind of cuisine
20. Ponder
22. Vetoes
24. Scrawny one
27. Hanukkah item
31. Santa Rosa auto museum item (2 wds.)
33. Buzz
34. Steakhouse selection
36. Cultural Revolution leader
37. Computer operator
38. Pavarotti, notably
39. ___ no good (2 wds.)
40. Always, to a poet
41. Botch
42. Basket material
43. Bench locale
45. Fill your tires
47. The brainy bunch
48. Lay turf
49. Europe's highest volcano

51. Wealth
56. Japanese cartoon art
59. Site of Devil's Cliff
62. Type of bear
63. Hat-tipper's word
64. At a distance
65. Shade of black
66. Units of resistance
67. Cause for intermittent windshield wipers

Down

1. Chip in chips
2. Joint problem
3. Ruler unit
4. It may be proper
5. Assistance
6. *Harper Valley* ___
7. Mr. Potato Head piece
8. Fancy
9. Go back to
10. Ryan's *Love Story* costar
11. Poseidon's domain
12. Ballpoint, e.g.
15. UNM's lobo, e.g.
17. Bush-league
21. One who puts you in your place

23. Hotel amenities
25. Axilla
26. Col. Sanders feature
27. Route 66 keepsake place
28. Come into view
29. Hide-hair connector
30. Yogi's language
32. Car part
33. Regretted
35. Nuts
38. Industry magnate
39. ___ *Today*
41. Summon
42. Jukebox tune
44. Kind of show
46. Assemblies
50. BBs, e.g.
52. Chowder morsel
53. Old 45 player
54. Terminal info
55. Database command
56. Big galoot
57. San Francisco's ___ Hill
58. United Nations agcy.
60. Sound at a spa
61. '60s war zone, briefly

Answers on page 144

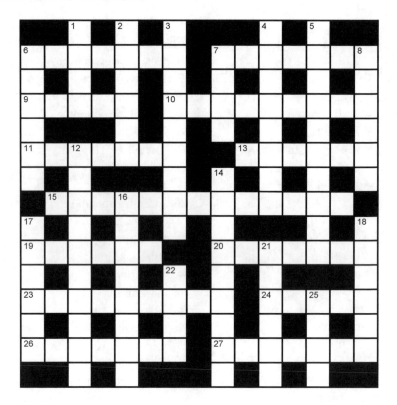

Across

6. Green-fleshed fruit
7. Redwood tree
9. Spin a baton
10. Jesus' followers
11. Chef's formulas
13. "Uranium City USA"
15. A precarious situation (2 wds.)
19. Route city: ___ Corners
20. King's chairs
23. One of seven fatal transgressions (2 wds.)
24. Your sister's daughter
26. School courses
27. Breathes out

Down

1. NE Arizona Indian
2. The "Indian Capital of the World"
3. Female deities
4. Tree climbing rodent
5. Dough flattener (2 wds.)
6. Shortens a hem
7. Give lip to
8. A pass leading to a basket
12. Quit an activity (4 wds.)
14. A spectator, often innocent
16. Unrivaled
17. Sour to the taste
18. Wedding seaters
21. Gallup Hotel: El ___
22. Poses a question
25. Ms. Macpherson

Answers on page 144

```
A V M I L A N M B W M E Q Z A
Y G C G A L L U P Q O R A N V
O H C N A R L E O V R E U C K
T E A F T U H S R B I G R I O
N U R O U A O U H W A N M Q L
O Q T S C E S M U L R O J T D
M R Y O U R R O Y J T J E T F
F E S T M O E T R H Y N F I K
Q U N I C H F U E A M A A W Y
R Q E L A T D A P N T S T E T
E U W E R D T T C O L N N R J
P B K U I R S A L L I D A P Q
C L I N E S C O R N E R S S N
B A R A P E S T N A R G X B T
F G K M E S I T A B S A Q M Q
```

ALBUQUERQUE	MILAN
AUTO MUSEUM	MONTOYA
CLINES CORNERS	MORIARTY
CUERVO	NEWKIRK
EL RANCHO	PADILLAS
GALLUP	PREWITT
GRANTS	RIO PUERCO
KIMO THEATRE	SAN JON
LAGUNA	SANTA FE
MANUELITO	SANTA ROSA
MCCARTYS	THOREAU
MESITA	TUCUMCARI

Answers on page 136

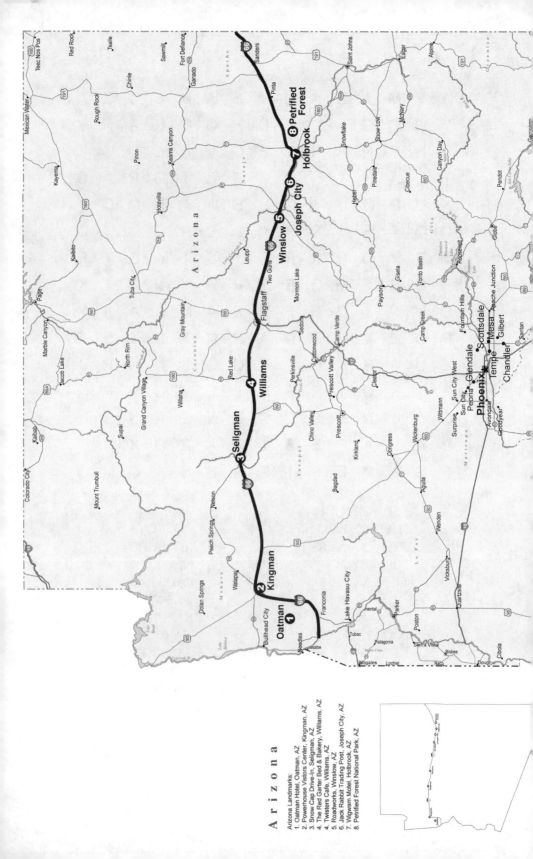

A r i z o n a

Arizona Landmarks:
1. Oatman Hotel, Oatman, AZ
2. Powerhouse Visitors Center, Kingman, AZ
3. Snow Cap Drive-In, Seligman, AZ
4. The Red Garter Bed & Bakery, Williams, AZ
5. Twisters Cafe, Williams, AZ
6. Roadworks, Winslow, AZ
7. Jack Rabbit Trading Post, Joseph City, AZ
8. Wigwam Motel, Holbrook, AZ
9. Petrified Forest National Park, AZ

Arizona

A deserted car in the Painted Desert in Arizona

Travelers looking for the quintessential western landscape will find it in Arizona. One of the most beautiful states Route 66 winds through, Arizona is filled with treasures. The Native American history of the state shines through, and there are many natural attractions, such as ruins, canyons, petroglyphs and caves, as well as more modern-day sites like curio shops, trading posts and even a wigwam motel. Visitors won't be disappointed, as Arizona has the longest stretch of Route 66 that is still being used today.

Houck is one of the first Arizona towns Route 66 travelers drive through. Its main landmark is its pony truss (bridge) that crosses Querino Canyon. The town also has ruins of the Querino Trading Post.

The Petrified Forest and Painted Desert are about 45 minutes west of the border, just off Exit 311. The Petrified Forest National Park features more colorful pieces of petrified wood than any other place in the world. Visitors can drive through the area examining one big piece of wood after another. The forest also has several Native American petroglyph areas as well as the Agate House and the Agate Bridge, which Native Americans built out of petrified wood. The park is actually two large areas – the Petrified Forest is in the southern area and the Painted Desert is in the north. The Painted Desert is a wide open space with amazing multihued badlands. Navajo and Hopi people have lived in the region for 500 to 1,000 years.

In the heart of Navajo Nation lies Holbrook, a town of 5,000+ residents. The town has always been a popular tourist stop given its prime location near the Petrified Forest. The main Holbrook landmark is the Wigwam Village Motel. This motel, opened in 1950, allows visitors to sleep in their very own teepee. The complex consists of 15 steel and concrete teepees, which are 32 feet tall (in the middle) and 14 feet wide. Each "room" has a bathroom with a sink, toilet and shower and features the original hickory furniture and two double beds. The motel closed in 1974 when I-40 bypassed the downtown area, but the current owners reopened it in 1988. Other stops in Holbrook include Tee-Pee Curios and the Historic Navajo County Courthouse and Museum.

Just west of Holbrook are two interesting souvenir stops – the Geronimo Trading Post (just six miles west of Holbrook) and the Jack Rabbit Trading Post in Joseph City. These shops have a great variety of items, including Route 66 memorabilia and Native American arts and crafts. The Jack Rabbit is known for its many black, red and yellow "Here It Is" billboards along Route 66 as well as the large crouching rabbit outside the establishment.

Jack Rabbit Trading Post sign near Joseph City, Ariz.

A few miles west is the town the Eagles brought to fame in their classic song "Take It Easy." Winslow has a girl in a flatbed Ford on its corner, so visitors often slow down for a picture. The statue is outside Roadworks Gifts in the downtown area. For those spending the night, the La Posada Hotel has been around since 1930 and continues to offer excellent dining and lodging. The hotel is in Spanish/ Native American style and was designed by the great Southwest architect Mary Colter.

Outside Winslow are several towns with interesting trading posts. The one in Meteor City features the world's longest map of Route 66. Near Winona visitors can see remnants of the Twin Arrows Trading Post, including the iconic red twin arrows hitting the ground.

Flagstaff is another popular stop for Grand Canyon tourists. Many of them visit Santa Fe Avenue (now named Route 66), staying in motor courts and eating in the cafés. Many of these buildings are still open, including the Route 66 Motel, the El Pueblo Motel, the Grand Canyon Café and the Museum Club (a vintage roadhouse). Flagstaff is proud of its Route 66 heritage and hosts Route 66 Days each September.

In Williams, Twisters Café offers some of the best burgers and milkshakes on the Route. It's a 1950s soda fountain chock full of Route 66 paraphernalia. This small town – often called "the gateway to the Grand Canyon" because of its Grand Canyon Railroad – also features Pete's Route 66 Gas Station and Museum. Williams is of note in Route 66 history because it was the last town to have its section of the Mother Road bypassed. It happened on October 13, 1984 when a six-mile segment of Interstate 40 opened. Route 66 was decommissioned the next year.

Just up the road is Seligman, a true Route 66 town. There are old motor courts and motels as well as classic diners like the Snow Cap, the Copper Cart and 66 Road Kill.

Angel and Vilma Delgadillo, who run the Route 66 Gift Shop (and barbershop), are two Seligman residents dedicated to preserving Route 66. Often called "the Guardian Angel of Route 66," Angel helped found the Historic Route 66 Association of Arizona. The Snow Cap is owned and operated by Angel's brother Juan. This is one of Route 66's most popular joints, famous for its tacos, milkshakes, red chiliburgers and jokes.

The Historic Route 66 Association of Arizona is located in Kingman. The group set up shop in the Powerhouse Visitor Center,

Red Garter Bed & Breakfast (& Bakery) at Williams, Ariz.

where visitors can get maps of the 60+ Kingman buildings on the National Historic Register and other information on the Mother Road. Also located in the Powerhouse Visitor Center is the Route 66 Museum. The museum traces the history of the Route and travel in general. There are vintage cars, service station displays, murals and life-size dioramas in this unique museum.

The rest of the downtown area hasn't changed much since Route 66's hey-day. Visitors should walk Andy Devine Avenue and Beale Street to see Mr. D's Route 66 Diner, the Mojave Museum of History and Arts and the Beale Hotel. This hotel is where Clark Gable and Carole Lombard married in 1939.

The last stop in Arizona for Route 66 travelers is usually Oatman. This town was once the last stop for travelers before entering California's Mojave Desert. Oatman is still an Old West town where travelers can see wood and tin buildings, Wild West saloons, burrows wandering down Main Street and "gunfights" on Main Street.

The Oatman Hotel is where Gable and Lombard honeymooned. It's not a fancy place, but it is full of charm – and possibly ghosts!

A Little Arizona Trivia

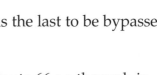

1. What rock group is best known for the recording "Take It Easy," which includes the lyrics "...standin' on a corner in Winslow, Arizona..."?

2. Which city has the highest elevation of any on Route 66 at 7,000 feet?

3. Which three Indian Reservations does Route 66 pass through in Arizona?

4. What mountain range is between Kingman and Oatman?

5. Which town on Route 66 was the last to be bypassed by an Interstate?

6. Which National Park does Route 66 go through in Arizona?

Answers on page 156

Route 66 Sudoku Challenge

Use logic to fill in the boxes so every row, column and 2 x 3 box contain the letters (and numbers) R-O-U-T-E-66. Solutions on pages 151-152.

		E			66
			E	U	
R		66	U		
		U	R		O
	66	R			
U			66		

	O	T			E
					T
		E	U		O
O		R	T		
T					
E			O	T	

Unscramble

Unscramble these letters to form a word or words related to Route 66 in Arizona. Answers on page 154.

AAFFFSTGL

_____

WWINSOL

_____

AINTPED EESTRD

_____

PEETRIIFD OREFST

_____

TTSSWIRE EFCA

_____

NAMGNIK

_____

Rock Shop at Holbrook, Ariz.

Roadside Attractions: Wigwam Village Motel

Holbrooks' Wigwam Village Motel #6 is one several teepee-shaped hotel rooms across the country. There were actually seven wigwam villages built from the 1930s to the 1950s, all of which were designed by Frank A. Redford. Two of the three remaining buildings are on Route 66 (#7 is near San Bernardino, California).

The first two motels were in Kentucky, and Cave City is where Chester E. Lewis first spotted the design. He bought the architectural plans from Redford and the right to use the Wigwam Village name, and soon built the location in Holbrook. Lewis operated the motel until 1974, when Interstate 40 came to town and bypassed Holbrook. After his death in 1986, his wife and children renovated and reopened the motel.

Today there are 15 concrete and steel wigwams. The white wigwams are trimmed in red. While there are no telephones or Internet capabilities, cable television and air conditioning are included. The original hickory furniture has been restored and gives visitors a good feel for what things were like in the motel's early days. There are vintage automobiles parked throughout the property, as well as green metal benches to relax on. Visitors often check out Chester Lewis' memorabilia that is on display near the registration area.

```
N P C F L A G S T A F F C T Y
T H A C K B E R R Y Z W Z E G
K Y T I C H P E S O J I N E W
N A M G N I K X O J S G O P I
O C S O A T M A N A G W Y E L
I C H A M B E R S V N A N E L
T W O G U N S D C A I M A D I
A S H F O R K Q D N R M C E A
V W I N O N A J S E P O O I M
R J A N A M G I L E S T N F S
E Z Z K O O R B L O H E I I C
S G N I R P S L O O C L R R J
E W I N S L O W A C A G E T V
R E T A R C R O E T E M U E X
L U P T O N U B N O P D Q P D
```

ASH FORK	PAINTED DESERT
CHAMBERS	PEACH SPRINGS
COOL SPRINGS	PETRIFIED
FLAGSTAFF	QUERINO CANYON
HACKBERRY	RESERVATION
HOLBROOK	SELIGMAN
JOSEPH CITY	TEEPEE
KINGMAN	TWO GUNS
LUPTON	WIGWAM MOTEL
METEOR CRATER	WILLIAMS
NAVAJO	WINONA
OATMAN	WINSLOW

Answers on page 136

Across

1. Time long ago
5. Rice University mascot
8. Field of vision?
14. Has debts
15. By way of
16. Noah's landfall
17. Teetering
19. Mother ___
20. Fit as a fiddle
21. Ref's relative
22. About 3.14
23. Stomach woe
26. Creole vegetable
28. Musher's transport
30. Rain hard
31. Yacht's headsail
33. Total
34. Barbie's beau
35. Fired up
36. Change of course
42. Fabrication
43. ___-Atlantic
44. Letters on a chit
46. Beyond control
49. The U of "Law & Order: SVU"
50. Ponder
51. Sty cry
52. Vantage point
53. Computer and telecommunications dept.

54. Usher's offering
55. Navy commando
57. Excavating machine
60. Tavern
64. Boring tool
65. Knight's title
66. Largest of seven
67. Winter vehicle with caterpillar treads
68. 007, for one
69. Job for a body shop

Down

1. "___ rang?"
2. Have title to
3. Hi-___ monitor
4. Book before Job
5. Race track shape
6. Like a gaping mouth
7. Set down
8. Town with wild burros
9. Get ready, for short
10. It paves the way
11. Anger
12. Dave in the Pro Football Hall of Fame
13. Strait-laced
18. Corn serving
21. Big coffee holder

23. Raises
24. Boor
25. Globular cloud
27. Home to the Powerhouse
28. Scrape
29. Permiting
31. Go downhill fast?
32. Will Smith title role
37. Baptism, for one
38. Classic opener
39. "You're fired!" notice
40. Roulette bet
41. Gardener's purchase
45. Beehive State native
46. Beat to the tape
47. Petrified ___ National Park
48. That guy
49. Dump
50. King with a golden touch
52. Sound at a spa
54. Taj Mahal city
56. Mysterious (var.)
58. Swelled head
59. Holiday mo.
60. Pack animal
61. Don't waste
62. Break a Commandment
63. "Dig in!"

Answers on page 145

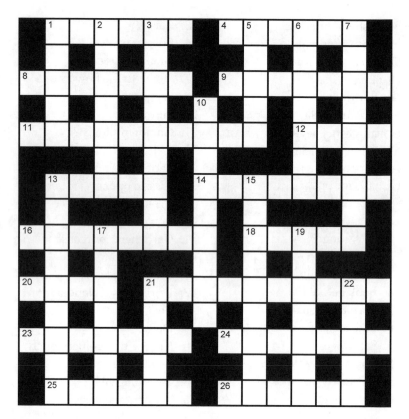

Across

1. Uses one's nose
4. Cuba's leader
8. Where you stand on the corner
9. Moe, Curly and Larry
11. Unsociable person
12. Golden Rule word
13. Stringed instrument
14. Junior, literally
16. American artist Norman ___
18. English poet John ___
20. Small bird
21. Jolly St. Nick
23. Junk email sender
24. ___ Desert
25. Jeter, Ruth or Mantle
26. Not convertibles

Down

1. Major Hindu god
2. Diabetic's need
3. Kenny Loggins' theme song
5. Thespian
6. Arizona ghost town
7. Travels past
10. Shining intermittently
13. A&E network show
15. Grimace (3 wds.)
17. Powerhouse Visitors Center site
19. Georgia's capital
21. Part of an act
22. Drug addicts, familiarly

Answers on page 136

California

Route 66's official ending point is in California, Santa Monica to be exact. The state takes travelers from the Wild West to the desert to the blue Pacific Ocean. But before travelers reach their destination, there are several stopping points.

El Rancho Hotel clock at Barstow, Calif.

The first place of interest in the state is Needles. This small town is located in the Mojave Valley and was named after "The Needles," a group of pointed rocks across the Colorado River in Arizona. Needles is known by many as the home of Snoopy's brother Spike. Peanuts creator Charles Schulz lived in Needles as a boy and thought the reference would be a nice tribute.

The first thing visitors see as they enter Needles is the covered wagon welcoming them to town. Other things to visit in Needles include the Palm Hotel, El Garces Depot and the Wagon Wheel Restaurant. The El Garces Depot was built as a hotel and restaurant to serve train passengers. Its most ornate side faced the railroad tracks and it was one of the Fred Harvey chains. It closed in 1949, then was used as offices until 1988. A group is trying to raise funds to renovate the El Garces Depot to its original glory.

Chambless, a bit west of Needles, sits in the Mojave Desert and is considered a ghost town. It was once a popular stopping point for Route 66 travelers who visited the Chambless Market, Gas (Station) and Cabins, but today the population is just six residents "and one dog," as the sign says as visitors enter town. The popular Roadrunner Café closed in 1995.

Ten miles down the road is the town of Amboy and Roy's Café. This café, service station and motel opened in 1938 and was a welcome desert respite for weary Route 66 travelers. Amboy is also known for its crater just outside town. Tourists often visited Amboy Crater for hiking just so they could say they saw a real volcano.

Amboy is a ghost town today, as are Goffs, Essex, Baghdad and Ludlow, the other towns Route 66 travelers went through before entering Barstow.

In Barstow, visitors find the Route 66 Mother Road Museum. The museum is in the Casa Del Desierto, another Harvey House hotel and train station. The museum has artifacts and photos of Route 66. It traces the development of Route 66 from its early days to today. Another Barstow attraction is the El Rancho Motor Hotel, which was built out of ties from the Tonopah and Tidewater Railroad in 1943.

Restored Claypool & Co. Building at Needles, Calif.

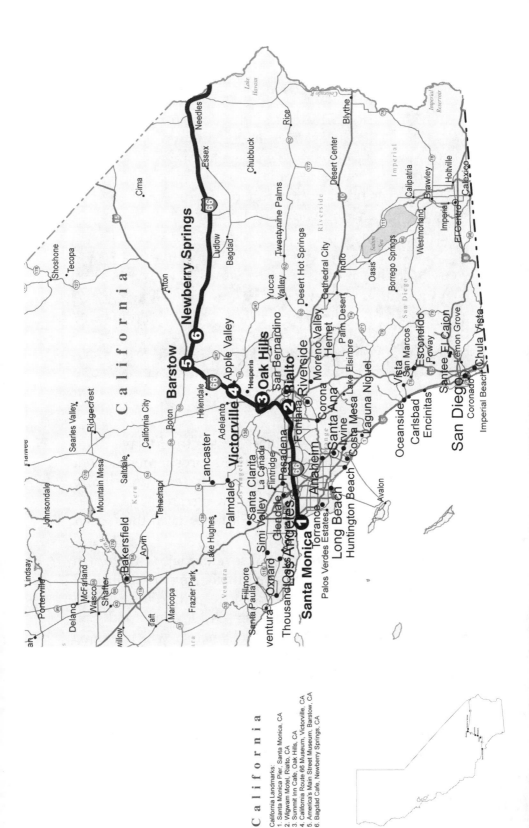

California

California Landmarks:
1: Santa Monica Pier, Santa Monica, CA
2: Wigwam Motel, Rialto, CA
3: Summit Inn Cafe, Oak Hills, CA
4: California Route 66 Museum, Victorville, CA
5: America's Main Street Museum, Barstow, CA
6: Bagdad Cafe, Newberry Springs, CA

Route 66 Motel at Barstow, Calif.

Route 66's steel truss bridge crosses the Mojave River as travelers enter Victorville. Once a prosperous cement town, the village had an Old West feel, and many Hollywood westerns were filmed in the area. Today it is home to the California Route 66 Museum, in the former Red Rooster Café building.

San Bernardino is the first of several major cities down the Route 66 home stretch. The Mitla Café opened in 1937 and has remained on the Route since. Still in the original building, the restaurant now serves Mexican food. San Bernardino is home to the first McDonald's, which opened in 1940. There's an unofficial museum on the site, where visitors can see paraphernalia that may bring back a lot of memories.

A wigwam motel, in the same vein as the one in Holbrook, Ariz., can be found in the San Bernardino suburb of Rialto. The motel opened in 1950 and used the motto "Do It in a Teepee" for some time.

Route 66 passes through Monrovia and Pasadena before visitors get to Los Angeles.

As they enter the movie capital of the world, Route 66 travelers will want to take a look at the Hollywood sign in the hills. The end of the Route was originally at Seventh and Broadway in Los Angeles but is in Santa Monica today. This area in Hollywood still has many movie theaters, cafes and businesses in the original 1920s and 1930s buildings. One example of the splendid architecture in town is the Los Angeles Theatre. This theatre was partially funded by Charlie Chaplin, whose film *City Lights* premiered there in January 1931.

Right outside Los Angeles and on the beach is Santa Monica, the current terminus of the Mother Road. Travelers head out of Hollywood on Sunset Boulevard and then hit Santa Monica Boulevard. The road winds through West Hollywood and Beverly Hills before ending at the famous Santa Monica Pier on the Pacific Ocean. Visitors should check out the Will Rogers plaque in Palisades Park as well as the art deco boutique hotels across the street.

Route 66 Sudoku Challenge

Use logic to fill in the boxes so every row, column and 2 x 3 box contain the letters (and numbers) R-O-U-T-E-66. Solutions on page 152.

	U		E		T
		T			
		E	U		66
O		U	T		
			R		
E		R		T	

				T	66
66			R		
T			O		E
R		E			T
		T			R
E	R				

A Little California Trivia

1. Where was the first McDonald's Restaurant located?

2. Where is the Harvey House train depot dubbed "El Garces"?

3. What river separates Arizona and California?

4. What desert is located on the Route in southern California?

5. What famous fault does Route 66 cross near San Bernardino?

6. Which city is home to the Rose Bowl?

Answers on page 156

Unscramble

Unscramble these letters to form a word or words related to Route 66 in California. Answers on page

AANST ACIMNO   _____

VVIILLCTORE   _____

WWAMIG OETLM   _____

HARYEV OUSEH   _____

EEENDLS   _____

AADDGB EFCA   _____

Answers on page 155

```
S  P  T  Z  S  N  E  E  D  L  E  S  O  O  M
W  A  A  Y  Y  E  L  L  A  V  E  L  P  P  A
B  L  N  O  H  W  N  V  P  W  D  C  N  L  S
E  M  E  B  W  C  E  I  A  S  A  R  O  A  S
V  M  D  M  E  R  E  G  T  C  E  S  G  B  E
E  O  A  A  N  R  O  O  I  C  A  M  A  Q  L
R  T  S  E  J  N  N  U  N  O  G  W  W  B
L  E  A  K  W  E  O  A  G  N  D  O  D  P  M
Y  L  P  H  H  M  S  E  R  A  L  F  E  E  A
H  C  E  O  A  G  L  O  D  D  W  F  R  D  H
I  E  T  T  N  E  V  C  U  Q  I  S  E  Q  C
L  E  N  I  S  I  A  L  U  K  A  N  V  B  P
L  A  Y  O  A  F  Y  B  A  R  S  T  O  W  V
S  L  C  Y  E  L  L  I  V  R  O  T  C  I  V
F  D  A  G  G  E  T  T  F  E  S  S  E  X  Y
```

AMBOY	LOS ANGELES
APPLE VALLEY	LUDLOW
BAGDAD CAFE	MONROVIA
BARSTOW	NEEDLES
BEVERLY HILLS	OLD STONE HOTEL
CHAMBLESS	PALM MOTEL
COVERED WAGON	PASADENA
DAGGETT	PIER
ESSEX	SAN BERNARDINO
FLYING SAUCER	SANTA MONICA
GOFFS	VICTORVILLE
LA VERNE	WAGON WHEEL

Answers on page 137

Roadside Attractions: Harvey House

Several old Harvey House buildings can be found on Route 66, two of which are in California. The Casa del Desierto in Barstow closed in 1959 and now houses museums  and city offices. El Garces in Needles closed in 1958 and is undergoing restoration.

These impressive buildings have an interesting history. A freight agent named Fred Harvey noticed the need for high-quality food and service along railroad routes. As there was no in-car dining and the cafés along the Route were generally of very poor quality, Harvey was certain profits could be made. He opened his first two restaurants in the late 1800s, and soon the Atchison, Topeka and Santa Fe Railway contracted with him for a system-wide eating house operation. The railroad provided the buildings, and Harvey provided the food and service. This is thought to have been the first restaurant chain ever.

The Harvey Houses were so successful because of their delicious meals, large servings, cleanliness and fine china. In 1883, Harvey decided to hire only females for his service staff. He looked for young, well-educated women to whom he provided room and board as well as generous paychecks. These "Harvey Girls" were known for their exacting service standards and became as popular as the restaurants themselves.

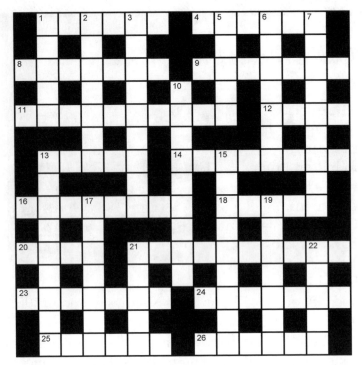

Across

1. Western terminus of the Route: Santa ___ Pier
4. Old VW model
8. Old TV show: "One Day ___" (3 wds.)
9. Chinese restaurant item (2 wds.)
11. Pizza topping (2 wds.)
12. Record a song off the radio
13. Provoke
14. Delegates authority
16. Second place finisher
18. Blender setting
20. Domed end of a church
21. Ballet dancers
23. Graduation certificate
24. Shoe maker
25. "American Idol" or "The Bachelor," i.e. (2 wds.)
26. Motel with teepees

Down

1. Motor inn
2. Observes
3. Bed covering, often
5. Debate
6. Mother Road Museum site
7. Common name for a liriodendron (2 wds.)
10. Hawaiian fruit
13. Colorful construction guide
15. See 11 Across
17. California's eastern-most city on Route 66
19. Colorful arc in the sky
21. Olympic basketball player Coles
22. Mr. T's group

Answers on page 146

The Torches Motel at Barstow, Calif.

Route 66 has been the inspiration for many artists. Songwriters, screenwriters and others have written odes to the Mother Road. The most well-known popular culture references are probably the hit song written by Bobby Troup and the "Route 66" TV show from the 1960s.

The song "(Get Your Kicks On) Route 66," written in 1946, has been recorded by the Nat King Cole Trio, Chuck Berry, the Rolling Stones, Perry Como and Tom Petty and the Heartbreakers, among others. The song most recently received airplay in the 2006 Disney/Pixar film *Cars*. This version, sung by John Mayer, was nominated for a Grammy.

The song lyrics include many cities along the Route – St. Louis, Joplin, Oklahoma City, Amarillo, Gallup, Flagstaff, Kingman, Barstow and San Bernardino. Winona gets its own special callout of "don't forget Winona," which helps the tune in its rhyming (with Flagstaff, Arizona).

The song was a pop and R&B hit for Nat King Cole, but it wasn't used in the 1960s TV show "Route 66." Producers selected a new song for the show, as they did not want to pay Troup royalties for his tune. The new instrumental theme song by Nelson Riddle became a pop hit of its own.

The TV show, which aired on CBS from 1960-64, featured Buz and Tod (and later, Lincoln) traveling

A mannequin hostess at Goldie's Route 66 Diner in Williams, Ariz.

America in a Corvette convertible. The show starred Martin Milner as Tod Stiles, George Maharis as Buz Murdock and Glenn Corbett as Lincoln Case.

The first mention of "The Mother Road" in literature was in John Steinbeck's Pulitzer Prize-winning novel *The Grapes of Wrath*. The book, which chronicles the Joad family's move westward after the bank foreclosed on their Oklahoma farm, was published in 1939 and became a movie the following year.

Unscramble

Unscramble these letters to form a word or words related to Route 66 in pop culture. Answers on page 155.

BBBYO OUPTR   _____

TAN GNIK ELOC   _____

DOT SELITS   _____

ZUB RUMCKOD   _____

COLNNIL SACE   _____

EETTCRO   _____

Go Figure!

Solve these math problems featuring the number 66. If you need help with a formula, check the hint box below.

1. If it takes you 66 hours to drive Route 66, how many seconds have you driven?

2. If your vehicle is 66 inches long, are you most likely driving a tractor-trailer truck, SUV or motorcycle?

3. If a bus holds 66 gallons of fuel, how many quarts of fuel does it hold?

4. If you've driven 66 percent of the 2,448 miles on Route 66, how far have you driven?

5. If you step on a scale and it reads "66 kilograms," how much do you weigh in pounds?

6. If it is 66 degrees Fahrenheit, what is the temperature in Celsius?

Hints:

1. There are 60 minutes in an hour and 60 seconds in a minute.
2. There are 12 inches in a foot.
3. There are four quarts in a gallon.
4. Multiply the miles by .66.
5. Kg times 2.2 equals pounds.
6. $(F - 32) \times 5/9 = C$

Answers on page 158

Route 66 Sudoku Challenge

Use logic to fill in the boxes so every row, column and 2 x 3 box contain the letters (and numbers) R-O-U-T-E-66. Solutions on page 153.

T		O		R	
			O		
U		66	R		
		T	66		E
		R			
	66		T		R

T					
			E	T	
		O	R		
		T	66		
	66	U			
					R

Other Famous 66s

1. Which of these New York City attractions is on 66th Street?
   a. Lincoln Center
   b. Empire State Building
   c. Times Square

2. Which of these countries is on the 66th parallel (north of the equator)?
   a. China
   b. Canada
   c. Italy

3. Who won the 66th U.S. Open golf championship in 1966?
   a. Billy Casper
   b. Tiger Woods
   c. Bobby Jones

4. Which century did the 66th Pope (the head of the Catholic Church) reign?
   a. 3rd century B.C.
   b. 7th century A.D.
   c. 21st century A.D.

5. Which city is the 66th largest in the U.S. (based on 2008 U.S. Census Bureau estimates)?
   a. St. Paul, Minn.
   b. Dayton, Ohio
   c. El Paso, Tex.

6. What was the storyline of the 66th episode of "The Andy Griffith Show"?
   a. The new mayor of Mayberry, Roy Stoner, is critical of Andy's work as sheriff.
   b. Aunt Bee runs against Howard for town council.
   c. Opie joins a rock 'n' roll band.

Answers on page 156

Route 66 Cryptoquote

The cryptoquote is a substitution cipher in which one letter stands for another. If you think that A equals Z, it will equal Z throughout the puzzle. Solve the cryptoquote to find a familiar Route 66 quote. HINT: Every M below is the letter Y in the solution. Answers can be found on page 158.

L C M T S R I R A K X E U N T

O T N T A P R V N , N A E I R X O M

P E M , N E B R N Q R Q L D Q P E M

N Q E N L V Z R V N . D R N

M T S A B L F B V T U A T S N R

V L J N M - V L J .

```
N  T  M  U  E  S  U  M  O  T  E  L  T  O  E
E  L  B  I  T  R  E  V  N  O  C  P  G  T  Y
O  S  P  H  O  T  O  O  P  E  N  R  O  A  D
N  S  A  A  R  H  R  V  T  J  A  H  U  O  Q
S  K  A  C  E  A  R  O  E  P  T  D  M  E  D
I  C  Q  B  N  L  P  O  E  M  K  S  Y  L  T
G  I  L  U  L  L  U  S  R  A  I  E  L  C  S
N  K  A  Z  I  O  O  I  T  H  N  L  P  Y  C
W  R  N  M  M  F  R  C  S  A  G  I  I  C  T
E  U  D  U  W  F  T  O  N  R  C  T  R  R  T
T  O  M  R  J  A  Y  N  I  I  O  S  T  O  E
G  Y  A  D  P  M  B  I  A  S  L  D  D  T  B
S  T  R  O  L  E  B  C  M  Z  E  O  A  O  R
H  E  K  C  D  A  O  R  R  E  H  T  O  M  O
P  G  T  K  G  B  B  E  T  T  E  V  R  O  C
```

BOBBY TROUP	MAIN STREET
BUZ MURDOCK	MILNER
CONVERTIBLE	MOTEL
CORBETT	MOTHER ROAD
CORVETTE	MOTORCYCLE
GET YOUR KICKS	MUSEUM
GRAPES OF WRATH	NAT KING COLE
HALL OF FAME	NEON SIGN
ICONIC	OPEN ROAD
LANDMARK	PHOTO OP
LINCOLN CASE	ROAD TRIP
MAHARIS	TOD STILES

Answers on page 137

Across

8. New Mexico athlete
9. Limo drivers
10. Kitchen appliances
11. Apes
12. Atoms
14. Got married on the run
16. Ice cream holder
17. Motel ammenities
18. Bonks
19. Headlight switch
21. Highway designer
23. State on Route 66
26. Slip away, as time
27. Emergency vehicles
28. Pronto in memo form

Down

1. Teaching method
2. Cruisin' car
3. Misbehaves (2 wds.)
4. Indonesian resort island
5. Policemen
6. Gas station brand
7. Complimentary
13. Light a Lucky Strike
15. Route 66 alternative
17. Lisbon's country
18. Bikers' headwear, often
20. Route 66 attraction
22. Lubricant
24. Pet food brand
25. Part of a foot

Answers on page 146

Well, if you ever plan to motor west
Travel my way, take the highway that's the best
Get your kicks on Route 66

Well, it winds from Chicago to LA
More than two thousand miles all the way
Get your kicks on Route 66

Well it goes to St. Louis, down to Missouri
Oklahoma City looks oh-so-pretty
You'll see Amarillo, Gallup, New Mexico
Flagstaff, Arizona, don't forget Wynonna
Kingman, Barstow, San Bernardino

If you get hip to this kind of trip
I think I'll take that California trip
Get your kicks on Route 66

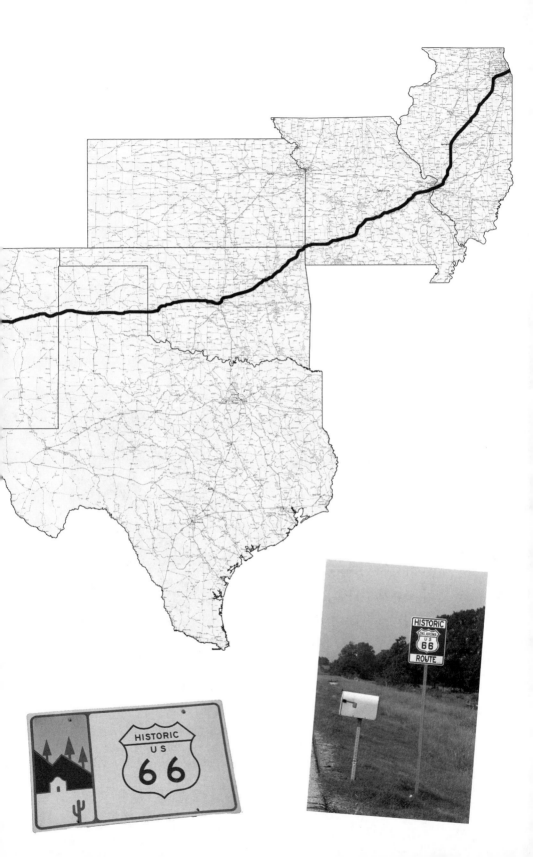

BONUS MILES

The Top 6 of 6 on 66

There are attractions for all tastes on Route 66. No two people have the same experience while driving the Main Street of America.

After covering the entire Route 66 (twice) the authors have compiled "The Best Of" lists for a variety of categories. The lists are completely unscientific and are not meant as an endorsement for any of the establishments. The order of each list is geographical, from east to west.

Enjoy these places, but enjoy everything else on the route, too!

Top Museums

- Route 66 Association Hall of Fame & Museum, Pontiac, Ill.

- Route 66 Interpretive Center, Chandler, Okla.

- Oklahoma Route 66 Museum, Clinton, Okla.

- National Route 66 Museum, Elk City, Okla.

- America's Main Street Museum, Barstow, Calif.

- California Route 66 Museum, Victorville, Calif.

The Route 66 Association Hall of Fame & Museum at Pontiac, Ill., has a great collection of Route 66 artifacts and tributes to restored sites on the Route. Located in a restored city hall/police station/fire station, the museum includes great artwork and a cozy gift shop.

The Blue Swallow Motel at Tucumcari, N.M., has been a fixture on Route 66 since 1939. It features individual guest garages, as well as striking murals on the motel's walls.

Top Motels

- Blue Swallow Motel, Tucumcari, N.M.
- El Rancho Motel, Gallup, N.M.
- Wigwam Motel, Holbrook, Ariz.
- The Red Garter Bed & Bakery, Williams, Ariz.
- Oatman Hotel, Oatman, Ariz.
- Wigwam Motel, Rialto, Calif.

Besides the famed 72-ounce steak, The Big Texan at Amarillo, Tex., has a varied menu, as well as an arcade and roomy gift shop.

Top Restaurants

- Cozy Dogs Drive-In, Springfield, Ill.
- Ariston Café, Litchfield, Ill.
- Johnnie's, El Reno, Okla.
- The Big Texan, Amarillo, Tex.
- Joseph's Bar & Grill, Santa Rosa, N.M.
- Bagdad Café, Newberry Springs, Calif.

Ted Drewes in St. Louis has been serving its frozen custard—known as a "concrete"—since 1929. The location on Route 66 has been in operation since 1941.

Top Desserts

- Ted Drewes (frozen custard), St. Louis, Mo.
- Midpoint Café (apple pie), Adrian, Tex.
- 66 Diner (milkshake), Albuquerque, N.M.
- Twisters Cafe (ice cream), Williams, Ariz.
- Snow Cap Drive-In (ice cream), Seligman, Ariz.
- Summit Inn Café (ice cream), Oak Hills, Calif.

The Round Barn at Arcadia, Okla., was built in 1898 and originally served as a home for livestock. In 1988 the roof collapsed, but in 1992 the barn was restored and now houses a collection of Route 66 memorabilia and a vast gift shop.

Top Gift Shops

- Meramec Caverns, Stanton, Mo.
- 4 Women on the Route, Galena, Kan.
- Round Barn, Arcadia, Okla.
- Jack Rabbit Trading Post, Joseph City, Ariz.
- Roadworks, Winslow, Ariz.
- Powerhouse Visitors Center, Kingman, Ariz.

Special Mention Gift Shops:

Joliet Area Historical Museum, Joliet, Ill.

Amarillo's Route 66 Store, Amarillo, Tex.

The Tee Pee, Tucumcari, N.M.

California Route 66 Museum, Victorville, Calif.

Honorable Mention Gift Shops:

Standard-Sinclair/Odell Gas Station, Odell, Ill.

Route 66 Association Hall of Fame & Museum, Pontiac, Ill.

Dixie Trucker Plaza, McLean, Ill.

Funks Grove Maple Sirup, Shirley, Ill.

Henry's Ra66it Ranch, Staunton, Ill.

Sherman's Curiosity Shop, Atlanta, Ill.

Jesse James Wax Museum, Stanton, Mo.

Antique Toy Museum, Stanton, Mo.

Voss Truck Port, Cuba, Mo.

Fanning US 66 Outpost, Cuba, Mo.

Munger Moss Motel, Lebanan, Mo.

Baxter Springs 66 Station Welcome Center, Baxter Springs, Kan.

Will Rogers Memorial Museum, Claremore, Okla.

Afton Station & Route 66 Packards, Afton, Okla.

Oklahoma Route 66 Museum, Clinton, Okla.

Route 66 Interpretive Center, Chandler, Okla.

POPS, Arcadia, Okla.

National Route 66 Museum, Elk City, Okla.

Mamie's Gift Shop, Stroud, Okla.

Allen's Fillin' Station, Commerce, Okla.

Lucille's Roadhouse, Weatherford, Okla.

The Big Texan Gift Shop, Amarillo, Tex.

Midpoint Café, Adrian, Tex.

Flying C Ranch, Moriarty, N.M.

Joseph's Bar & Grill, Santa Rosa, N.M.

Route 66 Auto Museum, Santa Rosa, N.M.

El Rancho Hotel, Gallup, N.M.

Holbrook Visitors Center & Museum, Holbrook, Ariz.

Meteor City Trading Post, Meteor City, Ariz.

Twisters 50's Soda Fountain, Williams, Ariz.

Sundancer, Williams, Ariz.

Route 66 Inn, Williams, Ariz.

Historic General Store, Seligman, Ariz.

Angel & Vilma's Gift Shop, Seligman, Ariz.

Ace In the Hole Gift Shop, Oatman, Ariz.

Classy Ass Gifts of Oatman, Oatman, Ariz.

America's Main Street Museum, Barstow, Calif.

Wigwam Motel, Rialto, Calif.

The Santa Monica Pier is the official end point (or starting point) of Route 66. There's plenty to do at the pier: food stands, curio kiosks, fishing, the beach and people watching

Top Attractions

- Grant Park, Chicago, Ill.
- Gateway Arch, St. Louis, Mo.
- Will Rogers Memorial Museum, Claremore, Okla.
- Oklahoma City National Memorial, Oklahoma City, Okla.
- Petrified Forest National Park, Ariz.
- Santa Monica Pier, Calif.

The Answers

Historic Route 66 Word Search, page 9

```
K B V P O M Z V A W M T R A V E L E R S
A D H O V B D L Y S V J M B D N S W P F
O C U T B C H T B L A E D W E N S B T N
R I B S B K N C Y F R N X V B F X R T P
A R L E T Z K A M I C G J C D C T H C F
D O E D B B K Y C N H F G P A V E N I Q
R T R I C Q O A X W I L L R O G E R S K
K S F S P O N W T P T K Y G R V R Y G N
C I B D V A N H L O E P M A C O T U A O
N H V A H G C G P L C O P S F X S K S I
G X D O D Z H I R X T E J S R U N X A S
V R L R E W O H N E S I E T H G I W D S
U N E R Z S L J L O S K B A S D A A F E
V P V E Z R V P F A M S J T S D M X H R
A K M H N V U W Z O G A C I H C L T X P
Z Q H T U I R E F X A U T O M O B I L E
J J A O M A G V S E L E G N A S O L M D
O L I M T M Q N W U I K E I A W H Z W S
K E T H X C Q A E C Q K V D P S L C J F
```

Illinois Word Search, page 28

Missouri Word Search, page 43

```
E  E  C  A  W  C  O  N  W  A  Y  V  Z  C  Z
R  O  R  S  M  U  A  N  I  L  P  O  J  L  M
E  S  I  J  T  V  M  S  Q  E  N  E  U  S  P
C  Z  D  Q  I  A  P  W  E  B  B  C  I  T  Y
N  E  A  L  V  S  N  O  N  A  L  P  A  R  S
E  O  L  I  E  C  N  T  Y  N  C  C  K  A  O
P  U  L  S  O  I  G  O  O  O  U  E  E  F  Q
S  L  H  U  T  F  F  K  B  N  B  G  R  F  W
A  B  Q  A  V  N  O  G  O  R  A  D  U  O  O
O  U  S  A  M  P  S  O  N  H  U  P  E  R  U
R  O  L  L  A  E  L  T  T  I  L  O  O  D  S
R  Q  D  O  O  W  K  R  I  K  R  D  B  N  M
Y  G  R  U  B  S  A  E  L  M  T  P  W  Q  D
E  Q  Z  P  A  C  I  F  I  C  H  T  S  I  B
E  O  Y  L  E  B  C  T  L  N  S  S  J  D  I
```

Kansas Word Search, page 49

```
B  S  I  D  I  L  I  Q  C  A  O  M  C  O  D
P  T  K  Y  A  K  E  E  R  C  L  A  O  H  S
X  J  D  C  J  O  X  T  W  Y  F  P  S  H  A
M  P  B  E  N  A  R  I  V  E  R  T  O  N  T
A  T  Y  R  O  U  T  E  N  D  Y  R  D  U  U
O  S  G  N  I  R  P  S  R  E  T  X  A  B  R
C  O  P  L  T  D  R  E  X  C  I  Y  F  O  M
A  P  A  O  A  M  G  E  R  A  C  A  O  S  K
X  N  V  I  T  V  U  E  H  R  E  W  U  I  M
E  G  E  Z  S  S  E  S  Q  S  R  H  N  I  N
T  I  M  L  S  K  T  D  E  Y  I  G  T  Q  H
A  S  E  R  A  H  K  S  I  U  P  I  A  U  E
H  V  N  F  G  G  E  B  E  N  M  H  I  J  J
C  I  T  N  U  L  B  L  V  R  E  C  N  C  B
V  P  Q  Y  W  Q  I  I  L  F  Z  R  W  I  O
```

Oklahoma Word Search, page 63

Texas Word Search, page 80

New Mexico Word Search, page 91

Arizona Word Search, page 101

California Word Search, page 112

Pop Culture Word Search, page 122

Historic Route 66 Crossword, page 10

```
P I E . G R A F T . R A T I O
R N A . R A D A R . E L U D E
I T S . A N O D E . M A N O R
M A I N S T R E E T U S A . .
E C L I P S E . . A S K F O R
S T Y E . R S V P . A I D E .
. . C R T . P E E L . S E T .
. S E I S M O G R A P H . . .
G O A . O H I O . S P A . . .
A R T S . I D L E . . T W A S
S T U P O R . . M A S S I V E
. R O U T E S I X T Y S I X .
H A D N T . L O G I A . E A T
A D A G E . M O R A L . U T E
T O Y E D . S T E L E . P E T
```

Historic Route 66 Small Crossword, page 12

```
. M . A . B . . D . R . J . .
S I N C L A I R . R E A G A N
. L . H . R . O . Y . B . L .
C A F E . B L U E R I B B O N
. G . . . W . T . U . I . P .
Y E M E N I . E I N S T E I N
. . . M . R . S . . . F . E .
. A B B R E V I A T I O N S .
. S . A . . . X . R . O . . .
S P I N S O U T . E L D E R S
. H . K . B . Y . A . . . I .
F A R M H O U S E S . T O D O
. L . E . I . I . U . A . I .
S T A N D S . X E R O X I N G
. S . T . T . . . Y . I . G .
```

Illinois Crossword, page 26

```
U G L I S . F A I T H . T I C
P A I N T . A N D R E . R N A
S Y N C O P A T I O N . I D S
. C A P E . S O W S . B U T
T W O S . R H Y M E . H U L L
R E L E A S E . L O U N G E
Y E N . K I W I . G L E E
. G R A N T P A R K
. L I M O . S U R E . C H A
T E N A N T . F I S C H E R
H A H N . H O O F S . L I M E
I R A . D E A R . E P I C
E N S . A S S A S S I N A T E
V E T . D I T T O . C I G A R
E R E . A S S E T . S C O U R
```

Illinois Small Crossword, page 30

```
. C E . T . L . L . O . G
C H A C H A . I C E C R E A M
. O . L . T . N . O . N . Z
R O M A N T I C . N E A R E D
. C . I . O . O . A . M . B
C H A R C O A L . R E E B O K
. O . . . N . D . N .
C O Z Y D O G . P O N T I A C
. . . O . D . C . . . D
C A R U S O . H A N D M A D E
. M . N . M . I . O . E . W
G A R G L E . C A D I L L A C
. Z . E . T . A . O . O . T
G O O S E E G G . F U D G E S
. N . T . R . O . F . Y . R
```

Missouri 66 Crossword, page 38

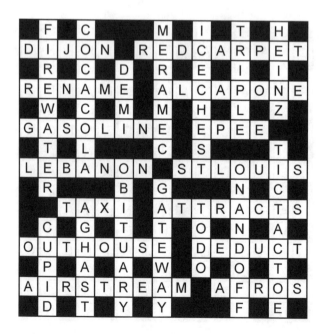

```
A D O P T   O N C E   I S M S
R O G E R   V I O L   C O A T
C O R G I   E C O M M E R C E
O R E   C O R K   S E C R E T
    L E A D     R A Y S
F R E E   R O A D M A P
R E L I C   G U A M   S P A
A N A   A B A L O N E   H E X
T O N   V E T O   C L O S E
    R E N E W A L   I D O L
  S T A R   P A S T
S T E R N S   B A W L   T A M
T I M E S H E E T   I M B U E
A L P S   M E T H   M O A N S
B L O T   O K A Y   E A R T H
```

Missouri 66 Small Crossword, page 37

```
  F   C     M   I   T   H
D I J O N   R E D C A R P E T
  R   C   D   R   E   I   I
R E N A M E   A L C A P O N E
  W   C   M   M   H   L   Z
G A S O L I N E   E P E E
  T   L       C   S       T
L E B A N O N   S T L O U I S
  R     B   G       N   C
    T A X I   A T T R A C T S
  C   G   T   T   O   N   A
O U T H O U S E   D E D U C T
  P   A   A   W   O   O   T
A I R S T R E A M   A F R O S
  D   T   Y   Y       F   E
```

Kansas Crossword, page 50

M	A	S	S		G	I	F	T		G	A	F	F	E
E	P	E	E		A	C	R	E		E	L	L	I	S
C	H	A	R		L	I	O	N		T	E	A	L	S
C	I	T	A	D	E	L		T	R	O	U	B	L	E
A	D	S		A	N	Y		H	U	T				
	D	N	A		W	R	I	T		S	O	P		
O	P	T	I	C		S	O	O	N		P	O	P	E
S	H	I	R	E		A	M	M	O		R	Y	E	S
L	A	N	E		P	R	E	P		P	I	A	N	O
O	T	T		J	O	I	N		B	U	G			
	G	A	S		T	A	N		K	O	I			
R	A	L	L	I	E	S		E	X	T	I	N	C	T
S	P	O	O	L		T	A	R	T		N	O	T	E
V	E	R	V	E		A	P	S	E		F	L	A	M
P	R	Y	E	R		B	E	E	R		O	L	D	S

Kansas Small Crossword, page 54

	U		K		L		O		F		T		H	
I	M	P	A	L	A		F	O	L	L	O	W	E	D
	P		N		U		F		I		L		R	
L	I	P	S	Y	N	C	H		G	A	L	E	N	A
	R		A		D		A		H		R		I	
T	I	S	S	U	E		N	A	T	I	O	N	A	L
	N				R		D				A			
A	G	A	I	N	S	T		A	R	T	D	E	C	O
			R				C		E				A	
N	E	B	R	A	S	K	A		N	Y	L	O	N	S
	R		I		T		R		E		O		D	
B	A	X	T	E	R		H	I	G	H	W	A	Y	S
	S		A		U		O		A		E		B	
R	E	S	T	S	T	O	P		D	O	L	L	A	R
	R		E		S		S		E		L		R	

Oklahoma 66 Crossword, page 64

```
V I A   S E R U M   C O B R A
I N S   E R A T O   O N I O N
T A T   M E W E D   N E R V E
A L I B I     E M S   D E W
E L R E N O   C L O U T
      L A P E L   A L A S K A
P A S T R A M I   T I M I D
O N O   H U N T S   O W E
M A Y A S   T A K I N G I N
P L A S M A   O N I C E
      H A Y D N   T E X O L A
O D D   S E E   S T R U M
P E A C H   L E A C H   A G O
U N D U E   H E L I O   T E N
S T A R R   I N L A W   E R G
```

Oklahoma 66 Small Crossword, page 68

```
  B   T   C   T       I
O V A L S   O B E D I E N T
R   C   H   P   S   D   T   T
E L K C I T Y   T H O R E A U
L   D   R   W   L   R   L
S P O T T E R   C L I E N T S
E   O       I   A   Z   A
  R O L L T O P D E S K
Y     I   E   P     N   A
U S E D C A R   U R A N I U M
K   G   E   C   N   T   E
O R G A N I C   C L I N T O N
N   N   S   R   I   M   I   D
  H O M E T O W N   A U N T S
  G     W   O   L   G
```

Texas Crossword, page 78

Texas Small Crossword, page 76

New Mexico 66 Crossword, page 88

A	G	I	N		S	P	E	W			R	A	S	P
N	O	N	O		U	T	A	H		M	E	L	E	E
T	U	C	U	M	C	A	R	I		A	V	I	A	N
E	T	H	N	I	C			M	U	S	E			
			N	O	S		S	C	R	A	G			
	M	E	N	O	R	A	H		H	O	T	R	O	D
R	U	M	O	R		F	I	L	E	T		M	A	O
U	S	E	R		T	E	N	O	R		U	P	T	O
E	E	R		M	I	S	D	O		O	S	I	E	R
D	U	G	O	U	T		I	N	F	L	A	T	E	
	M	E	N	S	A		S	O	D					
		E	T	N	A		R	I	C	H	E	S		
A	N	I	M	E		M	A	N	U	E	L	I	T	O
P	O	L	A	R		M	A	A	M		A	F	A	R
E	B	O	N			O	H	M	S		M	I	S	T

New Mexico 66 Small Crossword, page 90

	H		G		G			S		R	
A	V	O	C	A	D	O		S	E	Q	U	O	I	A
L		P		L		D		A		U		L		S
T	W	I	R	L		D	I	S	C	I	P	L	E	S
E			U		E		S		R		I		I
R	E	C	I	P	E	S		G	R	A	N	T	S
S		A			S		B	E	G		T	
	S	L	I	P	P	E	R	Y	S	L	O	P	E
A		L	E		S		S			I		U
C	L	I	N	E	S		T	H	R	O	N	E	S
I		T	R	A		A		A			H
D	E	A	D	L	Y	S	I	N		N	I	E	C	E
I		D	E	K		D		C		L		R
C	L	A	S	S	E	S		E	X	H	A	L	E	S
	Y		S			R		O		E

Arizona Crossword, page 102

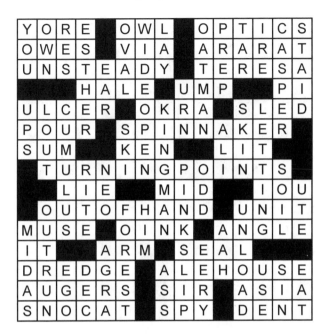

Arizona Small Crossword, page 104

California Small Crossword, page 114

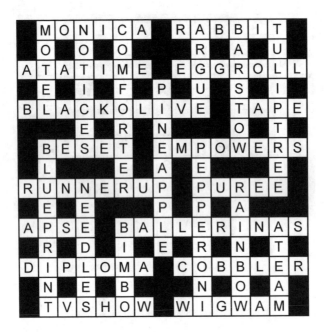

Pop Culture Small Crossword, page 123

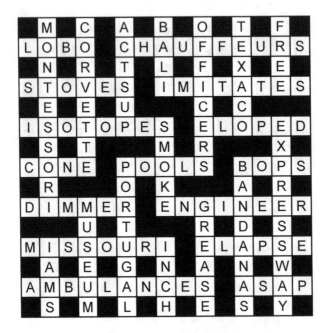

Sudoku, page 14 (top)

O	U	66	R	E	T
R	E	T	66	O	U
66	T	U	O	R	E
E	O	R	T	U	66
U	66	O	E	T	R
T	R	E	U	66	O

Sudoku, page 14 (bottom)

U	O	E	R	66	T
66	T	R	O	E	U
E	R	66	U	T	O
T	U	O	E	R	66
O	E	T	66	U	R
R	66	U	T	O	E

Sudoku, page 31 (top)

R	U	T	O	66	E
O	66	E	R	U	T
E	O	U	66	T	R
T	R	66	E	O	U
66	T	R	U	E	O
U	E	O	T	R	66

Sudoku, page 31 (bottom)

R	O	66	T	U	E
U	E	T	O	R	66
O	T	R	66	E	U
E	66	U	R	T	O
66	R	E	U	O	T
T	U	O	E	66	R

Sudoku, page 42 (top)

T	U	66	R	E	O
E	R	O	66	U	T
U	66	T	E	O	R
O	E	R	T	66	U
66	T	U	O	R	E
R	O	E	U	T	66

Sudoku, page 42 (bottom)

T	R	E	U	O	66
U	O	66	T	R	E
O	E	T	R	66	U
66	U	R	O	E	T
E	T	O	66	U	R
R	66	U	E	T	O

Sudoku, page 48 (top)

66	T	E	U	O	R
U	R	O	E	T	66
O	U	R	66	E	T
T	E	66	O	R	U
E	66	T	R	U	O
R	O	U	T	66	E

Sudoku, page 48 (bottom)

R	E	T	U	66	O
U	O	66	E	T	R
O	T	E	R	U	66
66	R	U	O	E	T
T	U	R	66	O	E
E	66	O	T	R	U

Sudoku, page 61 (top)

R	E	O	U	T	66
T	U	66	E	O	R
U	O	R	T	66	E
E	66	T	O	R	U
66	T	U	R	E	O
O	R	E	66	U	T

Sudoku, page 61 (bottom)

T	R	E	66	O	U
O	U	66	T	E	R
E	O	U	R	66	T
66	T	R	E	U	O
R	E	O	U	T	66
U	66	T	O	R	E

Sudoku, page 74 (top)

O	66	R	E	U	T
U	T	E	O	66	R
E	U	O	R	T	66
66	R	T	U	E	O
R	E	66	T	O	U
T	O	U	66	R	E

Sudoku, page 74 (bottom)

O	R	U	66	E	T
E	66	T	O	R	U
R	T	O	U	66	E
U	E	66	T	O	R
66	U	R	E	T	O
T	O	E	R	U	66

Sudoku, page 87 (top)

E	T	U	R	O	66
R	66	O	E	T	U
66	O	E	T	U	R
U	R	T	O	66	E
T	E	66	U	R	O
O	U	R	66	E	T

Sudoku, page 87 (bottom)

O	66	T	R	U	E
E	R	U	66	O	T
T	U	R	O	E	66
66	E	O	U	T	R
U	T	66	E	R	O
R	O	E	T	66	U

Sudoku, page 98 (top)

T	U	E	O	R	66
66	R	O	E	U	T
R	O	66	U	T	E
E	T	U	R	66	O
O	66	R	T	E	U
U	E	T	66	O	R

Sudoku, page 98 (bottom)

R	O	T	66	U	E
U	E	66	R	O	T
66	T	E	U	R	O
O	U	R	T	E	66
T	R	O	E	66	U
E	66	U	O	T	R

Sudoku, page 110 (top)

R	U	O	E	66	T
66	E	T	O	U	R
T	R	E	U	O	66
O	66	U	T	R	E
U	T	66	R	E	O
E	O	R	66	T	U

Sudoku, page 110 (bottom)

O	E	R	U	T	66
66	T	U	R	E	O
T	U	66	O	R	E
R	O	E	66	U	T
U	66	T	E	O	R
E	R	O	T	66	U

Sudoku, page 119 (top)

T	U	O	E	R	66
66	R	E	O	T	U
U	E	66	R	O	T
R	O	T	66	U	E
E	T	R	U	66	O
O	66	U	T	E	R

Sudoku, page 119 (bottom)

T	E	66	O	R	U
U	O	R	E	T	66
66	U	O	R	E	T
E	R	T	66	U	O
R	66	U	T	O	E
O	T	E	U	66	R

Unscramble Answers

Historic Route 66, page 16

MOTHER ROAD, SIXTY-SIX, I LIKE IKE, HIGHWAY, MAIN STREET, JOHN STEINBECK

Illinois, page 25

CHICAGO, GRANT PARK, DAIRY QUEEN, LINCOLN, RABBIT RANCH, FUNKS GROVE

Missouri, page 36

GATEWAY ARCH, MERAMEC CAVERNS, JESSE JAMES, STATE PARK, DEVILS ELBOW, SAINT LOUIS

Kansas, page 47

GALENA, EMPIRE CITY, BAXTER SPRINGS, SODA FOUNTAIN, MOTOR INN, CONVERTIBLE

Oklahoma, page 69

WILL ROGERS, TULSA, BLUE WHALE, SEABA STATION, ONION BURGER, MURRAH BUILDING

Texas, page 77

THE BIG TEXAN, CADILLAC RANCH, AMARILLO, WATER TOWER, MIDPOINT CAFE, COWBOY

New Mexico, page 85

TUCUMCARI, SANTA ROSA, ALBUQUERQUE, FAT MAN, CENTRAL AVENUE, GALLUP

Arizona, page 99

FLAGSTAFF, WINSLOW, PAINTED DESERT, PETRIFIED FOREST, TWISTERS CAFE, KINGMAN

California, page 111
SANTA MONICA, VICTORVILLE, WIGWAM MOTEL, HARVEY HOUSE, NEEDLES, BAGDAD CAFE

Pop Culture, page 117
BOBBY TROUP, NAT KING COLE, TOD STILES, BUZ MURDOCK, LINCOLN CASE, CORVETTE

Trivia Answers

Historic Route 66: Geography, page 13
1. Los Angeles, Chicago and Oklahoma City; 2. Mississippi River; 3. Adrian, Tex.; 4. Oklahoma; 5. Kansas; 6. Interstates 55, 44, 40, 15 and 10.

Historic Route 66: 1926, page 15
1. a. Calvin Coolidge; 2. b. 48; 3. b. Fidel Castro; 4. a. Harry Houdini; 5. a. *Arrowsmith*; 6. a. Gene Tunney.

Illinois, page 29
1. Lou Mitchell's Cafe; 2. Cozy Dog; 3. Eagle Hotel; 4. Steak 'n' Shake; 5. Dixie Travelers Plaza; 6. Rabbit.

Missouri, page 36
1. Mississippi River; 2. Concretes; 3. Eero Saarinen; 4. Springfield; 5. Jesse James; 6. Frank James.

Kansas, page 46
1. Route 66; 2. 4 Women on the Route; 3. Riverton, Kan.; 4. Sunflower State; 5. Home on the Range; 6. Lead.

Oklahoma, page 60

1. f. Yukon; 2. d. Tulsa; 3. b. Commerce; 4. c. Erick; 5. a. Claremore; 6. e. Weatherford.

Texas, page 70

1. Shamrock; 2. Barbed wire; 3. Groom; 4. Glenrio; 5. R.J. "Bob" Lee; 6. 72.

New Mexico, page 84

1. Texaco station at First Street and Route 66 in Tucumcari, N.M.; 2. Albuquerque; 3. Blue Swallow; 4. University of New Mexico; 5. Santa Rosa; 6. Dwight D. Eisenhower and Ronald Reagan.

Arizona, page 97

1. The Eagles; 2. Flagstaff; 3. Navajo, Hualapai and Chemehuevi; 4. Black Mountains; 5. Williams; 6. Petrified Forest.

California, page 111

1. San Bernardino; 2. Needles; 3. Colorado River; 4. Mojave Desert; 5. San Andreas Fault; 6. Pasadena.

Other Famous 66s, page 120

1. a. Lincoln Center; 2. b. Canada; 3. a. Billy Casper; 4. b. 7th century A.D.; 5. a. St. Paul, Minn.; 6. a. The new mayor of Mayberry, Roy Stoner, is critical of Andy's work as Sheriff.

Answers for other Route 66 puzzles...

Solution to 66 Box, page 17.

19	26	21
24	22	20
23	18	25

Historic Highway Box, page 18

There are several possible solutions. Our solution:

			O	K	L	A	H	O	M	A
				A	R	I	Z	O	N	A
			K	A	N	S	A	S		
						T	E	X	A	S
		C	A	L	I	F	O	R	N	I	A
	M	I	S	S	O	U	R	I		
				I	L	L	I	N	O	I	S
N	E	W	M	E	X	I	C	O		

Route 66 Wordsmith Challenge, page 13

SIXTY, SITS, ITS, SIS, SIT, SIX, STY

Less common words: XYSTI, XYSTS, XYST, TIS, XIS

Quote Box, page 62

Starting with the T in the sixth row of the sixth column, go down 2 squares, left 5 squares, up 1 square, right 4 squares, up 3 squares, left 1 square, down 2 squares, left 1 square, up 2 squares, left 1 square, down 2 squares, left 1 square, up 3 squares, right 1 square, up 1 square, left 1 square, up 1 square, right 8 squares, down 1 square, left 6 squares, down 1 square, right 6 ssquares, down 5 squares, left 2 squares, up 3 squares, left 1 square, up 1 square, right 2 squares and down 3 squares.

Go Figure!, page 118

1. 237,600 seconds; 2. Motorcyle (5 feet, 6 inches); 3. 264 quarts; 4. 1,615.68 miles; 5. 145.2 pounds; 6. 18.9 degrees Celsius.

Route 66 Cryptoquote, page 124

IF YOU EVER PLAN TO MOTOR WEST, TRAVEL MY WAY, TAKE THE HIGHWAY THAT IS BEST. GET YOUR KICKS ON ROUTE SIXTY-SIX.

BIBLIOGRAPHY

Books

Bernard, Jane; Brown, Polly. *American Route 66: Home on the Road*. 2003. Museum of New Mexico Press: Santa Fe, N.M.

Jensen, Jamie. *Road Trip USA: Route 66*. 2009. Avalon Travel Publishing: Berkeley, Calif.

Moore, Bob. *Route 66: Spirit of the Mother Road*. 2004. Northland: Flagstaff, Ariz.

Snyder, Tom. *Route 66: Traveler's Guide and Roadside Companion*. 2000. St. Martin's Griffin: New York, N.Y.

Wallis, Michael. *Route 66: The Mother Road*. 75th Anniversary Edition. 2001. St. Martin's Griffin: New York, N.Y.

Web Sites

www.historic66.com

www.legendsofamerica.com/66-Mainpage.html

www.roadtripusa.com/routes/route66/route66.html

www.wikitravel.org/en/Route_66